C000071986

Get Out Of
Debt

Hodder Arnold

A MEMBER OF THE HODDER HEADLINE GROUP

Get Out Of
Debt

Sarah Modlock
Edited by Denise Robertson

Ventures

Hodder Arnold

A MEMBER OF THE HODDER HEADLINE GROUP

Orders: Please contact Bookpoint Ltd, 130 Milton Park, Abingdon, Oxon OX14 4SB. Telephone: +44 (0) 1235 827720. Fax: +44 (0) 1235 400454. Lines are open 09.00 to 5.00, Monday to Saturday, with a 24-hour message answering service. You can also order through our website www.hoddereducation.co.uk.

British Library Cataloguing in Publication Data
A catalogue record for this title is available from the British Library.

ISBN-13: 978 0 340 94320 5

First published   2007
Impression number 10 9 8 7 6 5 4 3 2 1
Year   2012 2011 2010 2009 2008 2007

Typeset by Transet Limited, Coventry, England.
Printed in Great Britain for Hodder Education, a division of Hodder Headline, an Hachette Livre UK Company, 338 Euston Road, London, NW1 3BH, by Cox & Wyman Ltd, Reading, Berkshire.

Hodder Headline's policy is to use papers that are natural, renewable and recyclable products and made from wood grown in sustainable forests. The logging and manufacturing processes are expected to conform to the environmental regulations of the country of origin.

ABOUT THE AUTHORS

Sarah Modlock is a freelance journalist specializing in personal finance. Her first book, *Skint to Mint* – a money guide aimed at twenty-somethings – was published by Hodder Arnold in 2006. Sarah writes about all aspects of managing money, and her articles have been published in UK national newspapers as well as specialist publications, magazines and major internet websites including Yahoo!, MSN and AOL. She is also Contributing Editor for *Square Mile* magazine and has interviewed Chancellor Gordon Brown and Shadow Chancellor George Osborne. Before her move to journalism, Sarah spent nine years working in financial services regulation, helping to protect investors.

Denise Robertson's television career began with *BBC Breakfast Time* in 1984. She has been the resident agony aunt of ITV's *This Morning* for the last 20 years. In that time she has received over 200,000 letters covering a wide range of problems from viewers and from readers of her newspaper and magazine columns. She has written 19 novels and several works of non-fiction. Her autobiography, *Agony: Don't Get Me Started*, was published in paperback by Little Books in July 2007. She is associated with many charities, among them Relate, The Bubble Foundation, Careline and the National Council for the Divorced and Separated.

WHICH PAGE?

I'm just starting to deal with my debt.
Turn to page 8

I'm getting letters threatening legal action.
Turn to page 91

I want to go bankrupt. *Turn to page 102*

My partner has run up debts in joint names.
Turn to page 163

I don't know how to change my lifestyle to break my debt pattern. *Turn to page 3*

I have payment protection insurance – will it help? *Turn to page 69*

A loan shark has offered me money – I'm tempted. *Turn to page 86*

I don't think I can give up my credit card.
Turn to page 140

I have seen adverts for something called an IVA – is it right for me? *Turn to page 99*

CONTENTS

FOREWORD

By Fern Britton and Phillip Schofield

As presenters of ITV's *This Morning*, over many years we have met many incredible people with many incredible stories to tell. What we have learnt is that life can be wonderful but it can also be very hard.

Our phone-ins have generated thousands of calls a day from viewers all over Great Britain looking for suitable advice on a range of subjects. What is very obvious from these calls is that we are not alone with the personal challenges we often face and there is a great need for help in dealing with them. We are always cheered by the follow-up letters and emails from viewers saying how our experts' advice has helped them to turn their lives around.

Over the 20 years *This Morning* has been on air, Denise Robertson, our agony aunt, has regularly offered support and advice to millions of viewers on a huge range of personal problems and she spends even more time off-screen answering letters, calling those in distress and dealing with questions via the internet. As a result she is uniquely qualified to edit these books which reflect the common sense and sensitive advice that we provide on the show.

We believe these survival guides will help you to deal with the practical and emotional fallout caused by issues such as bereavement, relationship break-ups, debt, infertility, addiction, domestic violence and depression.

If you feel that your particular problems are insurmountable – don't! There is always a way to improve your life or at least get yourself on a path towards a new start. If you think you are alone with your problem – don't! Our experience shows that many of us face the same problems but are often reluctant to admit it. You have already made a great start by picking up this book.

We both wish you all the strength and support you need to tackle your own personal problems and sincerely hope that we can help through these books and through our continued work on the programme.

INTRODUCTION

For most of my life, until the last few years in fact, I've been short of money. Sometimes, through no fault of my own, the levels of debt have been severe, to the extent that I lost the roof over my head at a time when I had dependent children. There are few worse feelings than wondering where you are going to lay your head or find your children's next meal.

Nowadays, I smile to myself when someone writes to me about their own situation and adds that they don't expect me, with my affluent lifestyle, to understand their plight. If only they knew. So I wanted this book to be, above all else, realistic. I think it is. I wanted it to be a map that charted the way through the misery of debt to a place where life is worth living again. If you're deeply in debt right now, you may wonder if there is such a way out. There is, and you'll find it here.

Thousands of people have conquered debt and you can too if you seek help and follow a sensible plan. There are things you can do to lessen the amount you owe, find better rates of interest and seek more time to pay. All these options are covered in this book in a way that is easy to understand.

If you have had periods of not knowing where your next meal was coming from, you never forget. I still remember those 4 a.m. awakenings when I lay wondering if the gas would be cut off that day or the teabags hold out until the weekend. I know what it is to tot up what is in the supermarket trolley and then retrace your steps, putting things back in case you're short of money at the check-out. I can remember the numb misery of thinking it was going to be like this forever. Yet I also know that however deep the level of your debt, there is always a way out.

At the beginning, it can feel like throwing pennies into a pit so deep that you don't hear them hit the bottom. However, eventually you hear a chink and then the pennies build up until, eventually, the hole is filled up.

Some people can accomplish this on their own, especially if they make use of a book like this and fully understand their finances. Most of us need a helping hand. You'll find all the helpful agencies and sources you can trust to make things better, not worse, in this book.

There's encouragement here too, which you will need as you edge your way out of debt. When the going gets tough, remember that I was once where you are now and it needn't last forever.

Denise Robertson

Part 1: What to Do Right Now

1

Practical lifelines

Do you feel that you're the only person in the world with a worrying debt? You're wrong. **You're not alone. However bad things seem, it's not too late to get it sorted out.** There are people and groups who can help. Even if the banks and credit card companies are sending letters demanding payment, they want to help you make things better. The most important thing is not to give up. You *can* make things better and you *can* sort out your debt problems. Take a minute. Think about how good life will be when you're on the track to paying off debts and leaving worries and stress behind. You will feel in control of your debt and you will follow a path to a debt-free future. No more stress. No more panic. Start now.

Debt test

Answer these questions honestly, ticking any boxes which apply to you:

Do you:

❏ Have more than two credit cards with constantly rising balances?

❏ Pay just the monthly minimum for each credit card?

❏ Have long-standing store card debt?

❏ Borrow from one source to pay off another debt?

❏ Have trouble paying for essentials – mortgages, bills, food?

☑ Have loans taken out to repay other debts, which then accumulate more borrowing?

☑ Find that you run out of money long before pay day every month?

❏ Regularly miss loan repayments?

❏ Regularly pay for basics such as grocery shopping with credit cards?

☑ Face legal action by lenders?

☑ Dread the arrival of the post and put off opening bills?

❏ Argue with a partner over debts?

If you ticked three or more of these boxes, it's time to confront your debts and get your finances back on track.

MYTH: I can only afford to repay a really small amount each month. My creditors won't be interested so I may as well give up.

FACT: Almost all creditors will be happy to get even part of the money back and are likely to offer support if you show that you are willing to make some effort. Something is always better than nothing.

p 1: Get organized

If you are being threatened with any immediate
action which would put your home or belongings
at risk then it's time to get organized, turn to
Chapter 3. If not, you can start to take control of
your debt now. Here is what to do:

1 Find every letter and bill and any other money
   related paperwork.

2 Open all envelopes, however scary it may be.

3 Make piles of:
   • Credit card and loan statements
   • Catalogue and store card bills
   • Hire purchase agreements
   • Bank statements
   • Letters about your debts.

4 Put each pile into date order with the most
   recent on top.

5 On a clean sheet of paper, write how much
   you owe on each debt.

6 Next to each amount, write down the amount
   of interest you are paying on the debt (this
   should be on your statement).

Step 2: Work out the priorities

Next, divide the money you owe into debts that are priorities and debts that are non-priorities.

Your top priorities are:

- Your mortgage or rent
- Loans secured on your home
- Council tax
- Magistrate fine
- Existing county court judgement
- HM Revenue & Customs or VAT bills
- Child support
- Hire purchase agreements — Car
- Utilities bills
- Television licence.

These are debts owed to creditors who can take the strongest legal actions against you if you do not pay.

Your non-priority debts are:

- Credit cards
- Stores cards
- Unsecured loans ‿
- Overdrafts ‿
- Benefits overpayments
- Hire purchase agreements for non-essential items such as a television
- Catalogue arrears
- Anything you have borrowed from family or friends.

With these debts, you can't be imprisoned for not paying them and you won't lose your home, but if you make no attempt to pay and don't talk to these people to sort out payment, they may pass the debt to debt collectors and you could end up in court. Take as long as you need to sort out all of this properly.

You now have a clear picture of the money you owe so it's time to look at how much – if anything – you can afford to repay and who can help you.

Remember, you're not alone. The groups listed in Part 5, Chapter 19 can listen to your worries, help you contact the people you owe, and work through repayments with you. However, you'll need to be honest.

MYTH: I can walk away from debt and the creditors will give up.

FACT: If only life was that easy. The truth is that your creditors will do all they can – including taking legal action – to recover the money you owe, and it makes more sense to talk to them and agree repayments that you can afford.

MYTH: No one can take my home away from me.

FACT: This is not true. If you fail to pay your rent or mortgage or any debts secured on your home, then you risk losing it. If it's a property you own then it can be repossessed by the mortgage lender. If you are renting, the landlord can have you evicted.

Step 3: Work out your budget

The key to managing your finances effectively and avoiding debt is to draw up a simple budget – and stick to it. A budget is a simple way of balancing the books and making sure you only spend what you can afford. You need to know how much money is coming in and going out. It doesn't take long to work out a budget – it should not take more than about 20 minutes – and then you can see how much you can afford to pay on debt and where you can cut back.

1 Choose a time when you can have some peace and quiet and will not be distracted. If possible, sit at a table so you can spread your papers out.

2 Start with a blank sheet of paper divided into two columns. Use a calculator if you have one.

3 On one side, list details of your monthly income. Apart from your pay, this should include any benefits such as tax credits or child benefit. If you have joint finances, include your partner's salary but then don't forget to include joint costs and debts as you complete the next steps.

4 In the second column, write down all your monthly spending. This list will be longer than the other one, but don't panic. List essential spending such as your mortgage or rent, council tax and fuel and phone bills, and make a total of how much these cost each month.

5 List the monthly costs of everyday spending such as food, clothes, travel costs, toiletries, prescriptions and childcare costs in the second column too. Don't forget the cost of running a car (divide annual costs such as tax and insurance by 12 to get a monthly figure). If you smoke or drink, include an honest estimate of how much you spend each day. Then make a total of your monthly everyday spending.

6 Add the amount you wrote down for essential spending to the amount for everyday spending to give you a total monthly spending amount.

7 Take the monthly spending amount away from the monthly income amount.

The amount you're left with is the money you have that could be used to start repaying your debts. No one will expect every last penny you have, and repayments will always be affordable. If you have no money left and are spending all your income every month, then don't panic. You can still clear your debts. Start by looking at areas where you may be overspending. You may even find that your weekly food purchases can be changed or cut back, for instance by buying own-brand products and planning ahead so that nothing is wasted.

Reviewing your direct debits and standing orders is good financial practice, but it may also highlight things you had forgotten you were paying. Research reveals that, as a nation, the UK wastes an amazing £160 million every year on direct debits people forget to cancel. More than 80 per cent of people continue paying for a gym membership they no longer use for two or more months. Magazine subscriptions and mobile phone contracts are other items that go unnoticed. Ask your bank for a list of your direct debits and standing orders and make sure you review them regularly.

Part 2 helps you to look closely at where your money goes and to identify areas where you can cut back or make sacrifices. It won't be easy but you must do this to move on.

If you are being threatened with court action, bailiffs, eviction or the repossession of your home, don't ignore these threats but seek urgent help. Speak to a free, independent and confidential helpline.

Call the UK Consumer Credit Counselling Service (CCCS) free of charge (tel: 0800 138 1111) or use their online information at **www.cccs.co.uk**. The free service provides guidance and information on what to do (open: Monday to Friday 8 a.m. to 8 p.m.).

Britain's National Debtline can also provide advice and support (tel: 0808 808 4000; open: Monday to Friday 9 am. to 9 p.m. and Saturday 9.30 a.m. to 1 p.m.; **www.nationaldebtline.co.uk**).

For 24-hour emotional support, contact the Samaritans (tel: 08457 90 90 90).

2

Emotional lifelines

Step 4: Coping with your current situation

Being in debt can create many different feelings. You may feel:

- Scared ✓
- Ashamed ✓
- Guilty ✓
- Desperate
- Worried ✓
- Stressed ✓
- Lonely ✓
- Confused
- In denial. ✓

The way you feel may also affect your day-to-day life. Feeling anxious and distracted could impact on your work, your relationships and make it hard to sleep or eat. Coping with debt may make you feel depressed. The risk is that you blame yourself more and more, find it harder to open up, and the emotional struggle becomes harder.

If your emotions are churning because of debt concerns then remember: you can solve this problem. No matter how bad you think your situation, there will be a way forward and there is plenty of help available.

> *I always assumed that my debts were just too big to tackle, that I would never clear them and so it was not worth trying. Now that I am starting to pay them off, I feel so relieved to know that I won't have to spend my whole life worrying about them and feeling bogged down.*
>
> **Joanne**

Start talking

Once you take the first steps to sorting out your debt, you should begin to feel the weight lifting from your shoulders. Nonetheless, you also need to help yourself and put as much effort as possible into starting, and continuing, to turn your situation around. Talking in confidence to the debt counselling services (see Part 5, Chapter 19) may help you to open up and focus on a way forward. You can have an anonymous conversation about your emotions and feelings with the Samaritans who are available 24 hours a day (tel: 08457 90 90 90).

Be honest about your debts and seek help

The next step to financial recovery is seeking help. Ask yourself:

- Do you owe more than you thought?

- Are you worried about how you will pay off your debts?

- Are you struggling to make minimum payments?

- Is interest on what you owe mounting up?

If you answer yes to even one of these questions then talking to an expert could provide the help you need.

If you feel depressed or are having irrational thoughts, then speak to your doctor as soon as possible. He or she will be able to refer you for emotional counselling if you need it – something that could be invaluable as you work through the practical aspects of your situation. Don't be afraid to ask for help.

Open up

It is natural to turn to those closest to you when you have a problem and need help, advice and support. Yet this does not always feel easy with debt. In fact, you may want to hide your problems rather than share them. You're not alone. Through its work advising 15,000 people a month, the UK's Consumer Credit Counselling Service (CCCS) has found that more than a third of people in debt keep it secret from their partners and are more likely to tell their family and friends before they talk to their husband or wife. The organization found that women find it harder to share their problems than men. CCCS Chairman Malcolm Hurlston accurately describes debt as 'a lonely secret'. He says, 'It makes sense for anyone in a close relationship to share problems and we know from earlier research that relationship breakdown is a major cause of debt.'

Step 5: Tell your partner

One reason why it may be hard to open up to your partner is because your debt is likely to affect them. If your home or standard of living is at risk, you may want to struggle on and not worry them. Bearing this burden alone is not a good idea. However cross, disappointed or worried your partner might feel, they are also going to want to make things better, comfort you, and help you make progress. Many partners are more likely to feel let down because you have kept something from them, and may even be hurt that you felt you could not turn to them from the start. They may have noticed that you have been behaving differently. If you have been making a dash for the post each morning and your stress has meant that you have been less affectionate, they could even be worried that there is a problem with the relationship. It is not too late to turn this around.

Rather than waiting until things get worse, take your first practical steps towards becoming debt-free (see Chapter 1). This will mean that you can present a solution and not just a problem when you talk to your partner. It will give you both a greater sense of control if there is a plan to deal with the debt.

'Being in debt can be a particularly dark time', says money saving expert Martin Lewis, 'Many people are scared to tell partners, friends or anyone. But if you're prepared to take action the question isn't "Will I ever get through this?" but "*When* will I get through this?"'

It is up to you whether you decide to tell anyone else, but close friends or family will only have your best interests at heart and are bound to be supportive at a time when you most need it. You may be surprised to find that some of them will share previous or existing debt problems of which you had no idea.

The impact on others

When you accept help from one of the debt counselling organizations, it is strictly confidential. You will not have to tell anyone else about your situation, but the expert staff are likely to advise you to talk to someone close who you can trust, especially if the debt may affect that person. If the debt is from money borrowed in joint names, for instance, if you have missed mortgage repayments or have a joint loan or credit that you cannot repay, then you will need to tell your partner because they will also be liable. You can find out more about this in Part 3, Chapter 12.

The impact of your situation on others, such as your children, is something you should keep in mind as you work towards paying off your debt. It is natural to feel concerned about the impact of any lifestyle changes and how they will affect you and those with whom you live. No one can promise it will be easy, but there are ways to be more creative about how to get the most out of life on a smaller budget. You can find ideas, help and tips in Chapter 11.

Part 2:
Taking the
Next Steps,
Taking Control

3

Talk to your creditors

It's easy to see financial institutions as scary places that don't care and view you as just another reference number on a letter. In reality, lenders, banks and credit companies are usually very willing to help resolve debts and to compromise. However, this will only work if you talk to them.

The main reason banks and creditors (people you owe money to) send formal letters is because you have not contacted them when a problem starts, such as missed payments. You may also be dodging their calls and not answering their letters that ask you to get in touch. This makes the creditor think you are trying to avoid paying completely or even that you may be a fraudster. You can improve your relationship with your creditors simply by contacting them and staying in touch with them at the first sign of a problem. They will value your honesty.

Debt collection, courts and bailiffs – know your rights

Debt collection agencies

Your creditor may pass your debt to a collection agency. Don't panic or worry. Debt collection agencies do not have any more power than creditors – they are not bailiffs and have no rights to come into your home. They will contact you about repaying the debt and you can negotiate payment arrangements with them in the same way you would with the original creditor. If the collection agency tries to charge you a fee on top of the debt check to see if this is covered in the credit agreement with the original creditor. You should also contact Britain's National Debtline (see page 241) for help as they can advise on whether the agency should be charging the fee and who you can talk to if the fee is making it harder to pay off the original debt. There is always help at hand.

Harassment

Your creditors are allowed to contact you with reminders about repayments but they are not allowed to harass you or employ others to harass you. Threatening or harassing is a criminal offence. Don't over-react and don't hand over any money to make the harassment stop. Talk to the police or call one of the debt counselling agencies for advice (see Part 5, Chapter 19) if this happens to you. UK law says that creditors must not mislead you – for instance, by mentioning court action to scare you. Creditors should not try to scare you by threatening to talk to your neighbours or employer about your debts. If you are being harassed in any of these ways, tell your local trading standards department (see page 243). This department can also help with any questions about whether a creditor is acting legally.

MYTH: If I don't answer any letter or phone calls from my creditors then they cannot make me repay what I owe.

FACT: It is not that easy. Although you may feel safe for a while hiding from your debts, it's only a matter of time before you will be taken to court. Creditors can continue to act even if you don't respond.

Court action

It is understandable for you to feel scared if someone mentions court. It is natural to feel guilty even if you have tried hard to manage your debts. Don't worry if court action is mentioned. County courts are not criminal courts and the court is not just there to help the creditor – you have rights too and the court will protect them.

One mistake you don't want to make is to ignore letters about court action in the hope that they will go away. They won't disappear and you will end up making the situation worse by having less time to prepare because most letters about legal action give you a set time in which to respond. If you receive a letter beginning court action, there is plenty of help available. Britain's National Debtline (see page 241) has advisers you can speak to and it produces clear, helpful factsheets with all the information you need about how the process works and what you can expect. **You do not have to be alone during this process – seek help sooner rather than later.**

Bailiffs

A bailiff is someone who works on behalf of the courts and who can be authorized to take items from your home, which can be sold to help repay your debts. Bailiffs are not to be confused with debt collectors, who do not have the same powers. Always ask for identification. The bailiffs do not have to show you written proof of the court order but they will usually have this. If in doubt, check their credentials with the court.

Bailiffs may initially contact you by telephone or by letter to give you the opportunity to pay the debt. They are only involved as a last resort and if your creditor has taken you to court. It is important to know your rights when dealing with them.

Access and a change in the law

To add to the confusion, UK laws are currently changing. This section sets out the existing law and what the new laws propose. If you have any doubt about which laws apply, talk to your Citizens Advice Bureau (see Part 5). It is important to know your rights and to be clear about when you do not have to let a bailiff into your home.

The law in 2007 says that bailiffs have the legal right, in some circumstances, to force entry to seize your goods to recover the money you owe. This applies to fines, fixed penalties enforced by magistrates' courts or income tax arrears. For all other debts, bailiffs do not have the power of forcing entry to seize goods. If your debt does not relate to those listed, the bailiffs cannot use force to gain initial entry to a property. However, they can enter through unlocked doors or even climb through open windows, providing they do no damage.

Bailiffs cannot force past you into your home when you answer the door. It is important to note that once a bailiff has gained entry to your home, either because you let them in or they entered without force, they can use force to break into your home on any subsequent visits related to the debt.

The proposed new law says that bailiffs can force entry to your property regardless of the sort of debt, including unpaid credit card or loan bills. The timing for the introduction of the new laws was not known at the time of printing this book.

What bailiffs can take

If you are able to pay what you owe to the bailiff (and bear in mind that this is now likely to include the bailiff's fees), make sure you get a written or printed receipt straightaway.

If the bailiff gains peaceful entry, they will make a list of all the goods that have been seized. They can only take your belongings if they have the appropriate written authority, for example, a warrant issued by a court or, in certain cases, by a creditor. They can seize any goods that belong to the debtor apart from any tools used for work and clothing, bedding and soft furnishings 'as are necessary for satisfying the basic domestic needs of that person and his family'.

The bailiff is not allowed to take goods that do not belong to the debtor or that are subject to hire purchase or conditional sale agreements. They can take goods that are jointly owned by the debtor and another person, but if they are eventually sold they must pay the other person their share of the money.

The bailiff can remove goods immediately, and will usually do so where the goods in questions are vehicles. They will often leave other goods on the premises and ask you to sign a 'walking possession agreement' which means that the bailiff is now in control of the listed goods but is leaving them on the premises for you to look after and continue using. If you sign the walking possession, the bailiff can usually charge an additional fee. You will have a short period of time to come to an agreement to pay the arrears (usually five days) before the bailiff can return with the intention of removing the goods to sell at public auction.

Don't be intimidated

In the UK, the Citizens Advice Bureaux aim to help anyone who has questions or concerns about bailiffs. If you have experienced harassment, intimidation or threats, or if you have been charged large fees, talk to them about how you can complain.

The law on bailiffs can be complicated; don't be afraid to ask for help. Remember that you still have rights and, at most stages of the debt recovery process, there are opportunities to negotiate.

4

Work out how much you can repay

Whether you have one company chasing you for a debt or several, it can be confusing to work out how much you can afford to repay. National Debtline, the British organization that helps people in debt, has a simple solution.

1 Use your budget from Part 1, Chapter 1 to work out how much money you have left each month once your essential bills and priority debts (see page 12) have been paid.

2 Add your remaining, non-priority debts together.

3 Multiply the monthly amount you have left each month and can afford to pay by the first individual non-priority debt.

4 Then divide this amount by the total of the non-priority debts to get a monthly payment amount for the first non-priority debt.

It sounds complicated but don't be put off. The following example should make it clearer:

Calculation for repayments

£50 a month (what you can afford for all non-priority repayments) × £2,500 Blogs Bank credit card (first non-priority debt)

divided by the £4,800 total of the non-priority debts

= £26 a month repayment for Blogs Bank credit card.

Repeat this calculation for each of your debts and you will have a realistic and affordable set of repayment figures.

You should also consider ways in which to increase your income. If you can, take on extra work or sell any possessions to help boost your repayment power. Make sure you are claiming any benefits you are entitled to. In the UK, you may be able to get your council tax reduced if you live alone or share accommodation with a full-time student, student nurse or a person with

> *MYTH: I pay the minimum amount on my credit card each month so my debt is under control.*
>
> **FACT:** Not really. Paying just the minimum amount may be all you can afford but by the time interest has been added to what you owe, you are barely making a dent in the debt. To beat the vicious circle stop spending and start paying off as much as you can afford.

disabilities. Your local council or Citizens Advice Bureau (Part 5) can help.

Remember that your debt will continue to grow if your new monthly offer of payment to the creditor is less than the interest being added. Ask the creditor to stop charging you any more interest. They may agree to this for a limited period then start charging interest again. Ask them to waive any late payment charges too.

If you are not sure how to set out the payment arrangement you would like then Britain's National Debtline (see Part 5) produces sample letters that you can copy.

The hardest part was changing my lifestyle. I still saw lots of things I wanted to buy and was used to just reaching for my credit card. Resisting temptation, especially when I really wanted something, was so tough. What made it worthwhile were my bills and bank statements at the end of just the first month. Seeing my debt begin to shrink helped me to keep going.

Emily

5

Tackle each kind of debt

You have taken a deep breath and the first steps towards becoming debt-free and worry-free. Look how far you have come already. You have organized your paperwork and prioritized your debts, faced up to the situation and worked towards a solution. Keep going.

In this chapter, we look at how to tackle different types of bills and debts. This is so that you will know exactly what can happen in each situation and then you can get the best result from each company or organization with which you deal. It is important to remember that it is not just the people to whom you owe money that have rights; you have rights too.

Mortgage arrears

There are few things more important than the roof over your own head. Keeping up regular mortgage payments should be your priority before other debts. If you do find it hard to make the payments, it is never too early or too late to contact your mortgage lender and discuss the problem. Your mortgage lender can do far more to help you if you talk to them before things get worse. However difficult it is and even if you think you might be able to muddle through, you should get in touch and you will find that your lender wants to help. After all, it is simpler and more cost-effective for them to help you stay in your home and catch up with payments rather than take back the house and risk losing money.

Communicate

Get in touch with your mortgage lender as soon as possible by writing, phoning or making an appointment to see them. If the local office is unhelpful or difficult, contact the head office and try to reach an agreement with them. If you have not paid the mortgage for a number of months, it is still not too late to talk to your lender – contact them as soon as possible. It's also important that you start paying what you can, even if you can't afford the full monthly payment.

Know your rights

Mortgage lenders must deal fairly with borrowers and help customers in arrears by setting up a payment plan that is practical in terms of their circumstances and that covers the rest of the term of the mortgage, where appropriate. They are not allowed to put pressure on you with too many telephone calls and letters, but you can make the situation work as smoothly as possible by keeping in touch with them and promptly responding to any questions they have. If you think you are being treated unfairly by a lender, you can complain to the UK's Financial Ombudsman Service (see Part 5).

If you think you may be entitled to benefits, contact your local Department for Work and Pensions (DWP) or local advice centre. Changing the type of mortgage you have may also help you catch up – your lender will be able to explain any options available.

Don't make the debt worse

If you have mortgage payment protection insurance, find out how to claim. If you are really struggling, some mortgage lenders have rescue packages that could involve buying back part or all of your home so that you become a shared owner or tenant. Avoid the temptation to take out a loan to cover your mortgage payments. This will only provide a short-term solution and get you deeper into debt. If you take on any extra debts that are secured against your property, you will put your home at even greater risk.

If you have other debts such as bank loans, credit cards or overdrafts, your repayments for these should come after your mortgage and other priority debts. See pages 9–10 for more information about priority and non-priority debts.

Find a solution

Together with your mortgage lender, you can work out a payment arrangement that will also repay any arrears. Some lenders require arrears to be repaid within 12 to 24 months – ask your lender what they expect and let them know if you cannot afford the amount they ask for. If there are circumstances, such as accident, illness, bereavement, unemployment, separation or recent childbirth, your lender may be more sympathetic and flexible.

Don't panic

You cannot be evicted from your home without a court order. If your situation has become so overwhelming that you just want to hand the keys of your house back to the mortgage lender, then seek professional advice before you do anything. Britain's National Debtline can help (see Part 5).

Review your home loan

- It may be possible to move to a cheaper mortgage now or once the arrears have been repaid. Check what rate of interest you're paying. Lots of homeowners get their loan and then forget about it for years.

- Are you paying your lender's standard variable rate? If you are, you can almost certainly save money. If you're not, it's still worth shopping around as you could be paying less every month.

Rent arrears

All of the information in this section applies to UK tenants who started renting their homes on or after 15 January 1989. If you started renting your home before this date, contact Britain's National Debtline for alternative advice.

If you are a tenant and have fallen behind on your rent, check what sort of tenancy agreement you have. If you have an 'assured shorthold tenancy' then it is much easier for your landlord to evict you from your home. If you are not sure what sort of tenancy agreement you have, experts at Britain's National Debtline can help you.

Communicate

If you are having trouble paying your rent or you are already in arrears, contact your landlord immediately. He or she is far more likely to want to help you if you get in touch promptly rather than wait until things get worse. Ask for a breakdown of your rent account and make sure that all the payments you have made have been recorded and that the amount of any arrears is accurate. Use your budget (see page 12) to work out how much of the arrears you can afford to repay each month. Be realistic and pay only what you can really afford. If your landlord refuses to accept your repayment offers it does not mean you will lose your home. Keep paying and contact Britain's National Debtline for advice.

Rent increases

With assured tenancies and assured shorthold tenancies, there is no fixed limit on the rent. However, if your landlord increases it, you can write explaining why you do not agree with the increase or stating that you cannot afford it. You may be able to challenge the increase by appealing to a rent assessment committee (see Part 5). While you are waiting to hear from them, keep paying your existing rent and set aside the extra money if you can.

Know your rights

You cannot be evicted without a court order. If your landlord tries to evict you without going to court, harasses you or threatens you with bailiffs, he or she may be acting illegally. Contact Britain's National Debtline for advice straightaway.

Council tax

Most councils usually expect payment in ten-monthly instalments, but if you find that you are struggling don't stop paying but pay what you can afford. Contact the council and explain your situation and ask them to accept lower payments from you for a period of time. Bear in mind that if you don't stick to the new payment arrangement, the council may go to court to recover what you owe. You may qualify for a discount or council tax benefit – ask your council for details.

Gas and electricity

The companies providing your gas and electricity can simply cut off your supplies within a few weeks of non-payment. They don't need to go to court to do this. Therefore, it is crucial to contact your suppliers as soon as you think you will have trouble paying their bill. Use the budget (see page 12) you worked out in Part 1 to come up with an amount of money you can pay. This should cover the cost of the fuel you are using and part of any arrears you owe. Don't offer to pay more than you can afford towards any arrears or you will make things worse.

Shop around, switch and save

- Once your debt is cleared, consider changing suppliers to save money. Switching energy companies is easy to do. Start by making use of the free, impartial comparison websites that are accredited by Energywatch, such as SwitchwithWhich, uSwitch and MoneyExpert (see Part 5) – it will only take a few minutes of your time.

- If you decide to make the switch after your energy comparison, you'll need to fill in some personal details, which will be passed straight on to your new supplier.

- The switching process usually takes between four to six weeks.

Discuss repayments

All fuel companies should agree, under their code of practice, to accept manageable repayments if you are struggling financially. Advisers at Britain's National Debtline recommend that you keep paying what you can afford towards the fuel you are using, even if the company has not yet agreed to a payment arrangement. If you do not get an agreement from the first person you speak to at the suppliers, you should ask to speak to someone more senior until you do receive some help.

You can also ask the company to send you their code of practice, which explains your rights and how to make a payment arrangement. Most fuel companies will not disconnect you if you have agreed to a payment arrangement, providing you continue to pay for the fuel you are using and you are paying what you can afford towards arrears. The social services department of your local council may also help, particularly if you are elderly or have children.

It is important to check that your bills are based on meter readings and not estimates. Estimates may make the bills higher than they need to be. If in doubt, ask the company to visit and take a meter reading. The fuel company may ask you to have a pre-payment meter installed as a way forward.

Phone bills

As with gas and electricity, your telephone service providers (landline and mobile) can simply cut your line, without going to court. You must, therefore, contact your suppliers as soon as you think you will have trouble paying their bill. You can then refer to your budget to come up with an amount of money you can afford to pay.

Water

Since the law changed in the UK in 1999, water companies can no longer disconnect your supply if you are in arrears. If your water company is threatening to disconnect you, complain to Ofwat, which regulates water companies (see Part 5). Next, contact your water company and ask for a repayment arrangement. If you do not get an agreement from the first person you speak to at the suppliers, you should ask to speak to someone more senior until you do receive some help. You can also ask the company to send you their code of practice, which explains your rights and how to make a payment arrangement.

Benefit and tax credit overpayments

If the UK Department for Work and Pensions (DWP) thinks you have been paid too much in benefits such as income support, they will write to say how much money you now owe them. If you disagree with some or all of the amount, you can appeal but the rules are complicated. Contact Britain's National Debtline for details and guidance (see Part 5). Otherwise, the DWP is likely to make deductions from future benefit payments, apart from child benefit, in maximum weekly amounts. If this will cause hardship, you can request the DWP to take less money over a longer time or, in certain circumstances, write off the overpayment altogether. Your local Member of Parliament (MP) may also help negotiations if you are struggling. Tax credit overpayments should be dealt with in the same way, but your contact will be with HM Revenue and Customs. Contact them using the numbers listed on their correspondence to you.

Hire purchase agreements

Many different items can be bought on hire purchase – from televisions to cars. When you sign up to a hire purchase agreement, you do not own the item until you pay the final instalment. If you fall behind with payments, the company with which you signed the agreement can ask for the item to be returned so that it can be sold to reduce your debt. If the item is in good condition and can be re-sold for a good price, you will have less to pay. If you have already paid half of the payments when the item is returned, you will not be asked to pay anything more.

Q. If I sell the TV I bought on hire purchase, will I still owe them money?

A. Yes. Your name is on the hire purchase (HP) agreement and so you will have to repay what you owe, even if you have sold the item.

Credit debts including cards, loans and catalogues

The best way to avoid debts growing and the problem becoming worse is to talk to the card issuer or bank to whom you owe money. If you are struggling to make minimum repayments, you will sink deeper into debt and be slapped with late payment charges on top. Don't wait until things get this bad before you get in touch and talk about it. Using your budget (see page 12) and the system for working out how much you can afford to repay, suggest a payment arrangement.

Q. All credit cards and loans are pretty much the same.

A. This couldn't be further from the truth. Don't accept the first offer through the post or from your bank. Shop around and compare APRs to make sure you pay as little interest as possible.

Discuss repayments

If your creditor refuses the payment arrangement you propose, stay calm and don't give up. Britain's National Debtline recommends that you start paying the amount you have offered anyway as a gesture of goodwill, and then write to the creditor again to ask them to reconsider. Explain that your offer is reasonable and is all you can afford to pay. If some creditors have accepted your payment arrangement, then tell other creditors about this. National Debtline can provide further advice if these steps do not work.

Q. What is a consolidation loan?

A. This is money you can borrow to roll all your debts into one. The loan company pays the people you owe, then you make payments on one debt to one company. Make sure you know how much interest you will be charged and beware of rolling unsecured debts into a secured debt. A secured debt means that if you fail to repay it, the property you own can be sold. Think carefully before taking on more debt. See page 76 for further information.

Freeze the interest

Remember that your debt will continue to grow if your new monthly offer of payment to the creditor is less than the interest being added. Ask the creditor to stop charging you any more interest. They may agree to this for a limited period then start charging interest again. Ask them to waive any late payment charges too. Once they agree, double-check your statements when they arrive to make sure that interest is not being charged again.

If you are struggling

We have talked about the need to repay priority debts such as your rent or mortgage and utilities bills before you repay non-priority debts such as credit cards (more information on different types of debts can be found on pages 9–10). We have also looked at how to work out your budget (see page 12) and work out how much you can afford to repay (see pages 13–14). If you follow these steps but find that you do not have enough money or any money left to repay credit debts after you have taken care of your priority debts, there are still things you can do. If you have nothing left, talk to your creditors, send them copies of your budget to support your position and ask them to hold any action until your circumstances improve. If you have plans to increase your income, explain this to them and give an estimate of when this might happen, if you can. You can also offer a token payment of £1 a month to show good will. Throughout all this, if you keep communicating and showing your creditor that you are doing your best to pay them, they should be as helpful and flexible as they can. If you are still not getting anywhere after trying all of this, speak to Britain's National Debtline for advice on what to do next.

Understand how credit interest, fees and charges work

All lenders have to tell you what the Annual Percentage Rate (APR) is on any credit offer before you sign an agreement. The amount will vary from lender to lender. For example, if you leave £500 of debt on your credit card for a year at an APR of 18.9 per cent, you will end up paying an additional £94.49 to the card issuer in interest charges. Remember, your card issuer will be happy if you keep a large balance on your card and pay them interest. If you are looking around for a credit card or loan, you want the lowest APR rate possible. However, make sure you know what other costs apply – read the small print for details of any application or administration fees, legal fees or penalties that you will face if you want to pay off your loan early.

If you find a deal with a low APR, ask the lender the following questions:

• **Does the interest included in the APR vary or is the rate fixed?**

If the rate is variable, your repayments could go up or go down. If the rate is fixed, your repayments will stay the same.

• **Are there any charges that are not included in the APR?**

This could include charges for services such as optional payment protection insurance. If so, make sure you understand what the charges are, whether you really need the services offered, how much you would have to pay, and when you would have to pay.

• **What are the conditions of the loan or credit and do they suit you?**

For example, do you have a choice about how and where you make the repayments? If you suddenly have spare money, can you pay the loan off early and without penalties?

- **Can you afford the monthly payments?**

A more expensive loan (with a higher APR) could have lower monthly payments if they are spread out over a longer period of time. That might suit you better if your budget is tight, even though you would pay more in the long run.

Late payment and over-limit charges

Late payment and over-the-limit charges are made by most lenders. Imagine paying your bill but missing the payment date by one day and finding that the subsequent late payment charge pushes you over your credit limit to yet another charge. Expect to pay around £20–£25 for each. Avoid these charges by being clear about your payment date and meeting it in good time. Some banks take several days to transfer cash from your account to the card issuer, even though the cash disappears from your bank account as soon as you make the payment.

> *Q. My credit card company keeps raising my credit limit because it says I am a valued customer. Surely that means it's OK to spend more?*
>
> **A.** No, it means that the credit card company is making money out of you if you do not pay off your card balance in full every month. If they raise your limit automatically, call to ask for it to be reduced.

Avoid cash advances

One of the fastest ways to throw your money away is to use your credit card to make withdrawals at the cashpoint – also known as a 'cash advance'. You can withdraw cash using most credit cards provided you have a PIN (personal identification number), but instead of having an interest-free period of between 49 and 59 days before interest is charged, as you do with purchases, cash withdrawals attract interest immediately and at a much higher rate of interest than your purchase rate. Cash withdrawals also incur a handling fee or service charge, which tends to be a percentage of the amount taken out and is usually around 1.5 per cent for each transaction, although some banks charge a flat fee as well as, or instead of, this.

Remember to keep saying no

- It's crucial to remember that your credit card limit is not your money. You're borrowing the money and will have to pay it back, probably with interest. So when letters arrive in the post offering you loans or new credit cards, these are not opportunities to buy things you can't afford. They're the route to more debt.

- However much you feel you can't get the things you want in life without stretching your debt just a little further, this will make you miserable in the long run. Taking on more debt is not a way out. It will push your chances of ever getting straight even further away. When new offers of credit arrive in the post, don't even open them, but shred them or tear them into small pieces.

Repaying your loan early

You would think that if you borrow money, the lender would be pleased to have it repaid early. Although this might be true if you borrow from a friend, it is not the case with loan companies. Not only do they prefer you to pay over the time agreed, but many will charge a penalty fee if you want to repay your loan early. This is known as an 'early redemption' penalty or fee but may also be described in the small print as a 'redemption charge' or 'financial penalty'.

An early redemption penalty is usually equivalent to one or two months' interest. The earlier you repay the loan, the higher the charge will be. This is because the interest part of the loan repayment makes up a higher proportion of the repayment the earlier in the loan term it is. An early repayment penalty can add a considerable cost to your loan. Even if you roll the loan into another consolidation loan, you will still have to pay up if the penalties apply to your contract.

If you took out a fixed rate loan on or after 31 May 2005, new UK laws mean that as long as you follow certain procedures and meet certain conditions, you can only be asked to pay a maximum of two months' interest if you want to repay early. If your loan is older, you are likely to be stuck with the penalty if you want to get out of it early. If you have yet to take out a loan, there are now plenty of competitive lenders who no longer charge a fee for early repayment – think about this when you consider paying off existing loans.

Payment protection insurance (PPI)

PPI is designed to work in two ways – it will usually pay off your loan completely if you die or if you are diagnosed with a major illness like cancer, a stroke or a heart attack. It will also cover your loan repayments for a set period of time if you are unable to pay them because of accident, sickness or unemployment. If you are claiming because of illness, most policies pay out when you are too sick to do your job, although some specify that you need to be too sick to do any job – an important difference. You will usually need to be off work sick for more than two weeks before the policy will kick in, and then most policies cover loan repayments for up to five years, but check the details so you know exactly what is covered. If you resign or get sacked, the policy will not pay out. Policies do vary so it is important to read the small print carefully.

Almost all lenders give you the opportunity to take out PPI. It can provide peace of mind, but it is not cheap and if you decide you need it, make sure you shop around for the best deal. You do not have to take the PPI offered by the lender. PPI cover may be automatically included in your loan – research shows that nine out of ten high-street lenders do this – but that does not mean you must have it. Think about your specific circumstances before you decide whether you need cover. Check whether it has been added to your loan and ask for it to be removed if you do not need it.

Q. Do I have to take out payment protection insurance with a credit card or loan?

A. You don't have to but you may want to if you are not sure how you will make repayments if you are ill or unemployed for some time. Read the small print so that you know exactly when and for how long the insurance will pay out.

If you are not sure whether you need PPI, answer the following questions:

- If you lost your job unexpectedly, would your credit card bill or existing balance or loan become a burden you would be unable to manage?

- If you were injured or sick for so long that you had to take reduced pay or if you were on maternity leave, would you be able to manage your credit card bills or loan repayments?

If you answered yes to either of these scenarios, PPI may ease your worries but do read the paperwork carefully before you sign and shop around for the best value cover.

MYTH: I have payment protection insurance on my loans and credit cards so I don't need to worry about repayments if I run up debt.

FACT: Payment protection insurance (PPI) is designed to cover some of your debt for a limited time if you are unable to make repayments because you are ill or become unemployed. It has many conditions and rules, and may not start paying out until you have been ill or out of work for several weeks. It will not cover your debt simply because you have spent more than you can afford to repay. Make sure you read the small print if you sign up for it.

6

Think before you sign up to more debt

When you are in debt, it is easy to feel trapped and look for solutions that will ease your mind and get creditors off your back, if only to give you a breathing space. One big temptation is to sign up for a new loan or overdraft to pay off one you already have, but is this the right answer? There are many loans on offer that are designed for people already in debt. They offer the chance to roll all your debts together into one loan with one monthly repayment. These are called 'consolidation loans'.

Consolidation loans

These lump sums can be borrowed from banks, building societies and loan companies. Choosing the right loan depends on how much you want to borrow and for how long. The key is always to only borrow what you can afford or you run the risk of making your debts worse. These loans are also available from debt management companies that may also offer additional support in handling your creditors.

However, there are plenty of pitfalls to consider whether you opt to take out a consolidation loan or to sign up for the debt management as well. Most debt management companies will only take you on if you have some available income and own your own home. This is so that your home can be used as security against your debts. This means that 'unsecured' credit card or loan debts suddenly become 'secured' against your home. Put simply, if you fail to make the repayments, you could lose your home.

Ongoing problems

If you need help with priority debts, such as your mortgage or rent, any loans secured on your home, council tax, child support, hire purchase plans or utilities costs, most debt management companies will *not* be able to help although they may take you on as a customer for non-priority debts such as loans and credit. This means that if your debt problem includes not being able to pay your rent as well as overdue credit card bills, the debt manager will concentrate on the credit cards and the more crucial issue of the roof over your head may be neglected.

A debt management company should start by taking an in-depth look at your finances, including your income, essential outgoings and all debts. Only then will they be able to work out a realistic programme of repayment so that you can shake off your debt. If they do not take enough care with their checks, you are at risk of signing up to an agreement that is then difficult or impossible to keep to and which defeats the whole object.

Debt managers do not generally provide financial advice so you may not be aware of all the options open to you and the advantages and disadvantages of each. This also means that debt managers will not highlight any state benefits you may be entitled to so you will need to do your own research. You will also have to do your homework on the interest rate you pay on the newly consolidated loan. It will almost certainly be higher than your mortgage interest rate – it could be five or six times as much or even higher. Moreover, you are paying for a service that provides nothing you could not do for yourself or arrange for free.

The cost of consolidation

In addition to the interest on the consolidation loan, consider the payment schedule. It may bring a sigh of relief to see that your debt can now be repaid over ten years instead of two, but the debt manager is not doing this out of kindness – it is a way of making more money out of you.

One of the biggest problems with debt management companies is that they charge a fee. This is usually around £200, and there may also be an initial 'deposit'. On top of this, expect to pay for the distribution of payments to creditors, which may cost up to £30 per month. Before you sign any agreement, check whether you can cancel at any time if you are not happy with the service and if you will get your deposit back. It is essential to read the small print.

It is important to know that debt

management companies cannot guarantee a favourable outcome for you. You still need to do the work and keep up the payments. Just because a debt manager is involved does not mean that your creditors are obliged to reduce payments or freeze interest – they will only do this at their discretion.

Having a debt manager will not prevent creditors taking court action against you either. In fact, some creditors refuse to deal with debt management companies and so you will still have to maintain communication. Be very wary if your debt manager advises you to sever all contact with your creditors and pass on any correspondence to them. This may result in creditors taking action – including court action – against you which you do not know about.

If you still think debt consolidation and management is the way forward, you can get a free service from Payplan, an independent company funded by the UK credit industry. Payplan is one of the UK's leading debt management companies and its services are free. It can help you to set up and keep to a manageable repayment plan for your debts and undertake regular reviews of your circumstances to ensure that your Payplan arrangement is still working. The arrangement then continues until all of your debts are cleared (see Part 5).

Unsecured and secured borrowing

When you borrow money, the company lending it to you will want some reassurance that you can repay it over time. In some cases, they will look at your credit record (see Chapter 13), which will show whether you have a good history of repaying previous loans and lines of credit. If you are borrowing a large amount, they may want to know that you have something more concrete – literally, your house – which you could sell if you failed to repay what you owe.

Unsecured loans

If you do not wish to secure the loan against your property – or you do not own property – then unsecured loans are a popular way to borrow. As with credit cards, the key to the cost of your loan is determined by the Annual Percentage Rate (APR), which relates to the interest you pay on the cash you borrow. The interest can be charged at a fixed or variable rate. All lenders must show clearly what the APR rate for any loan is so that borrowers can compare products and see the true rate of interest they will pay.

Borrow only what you can afford, even if you're offered more. Aim to pay the money back in as short a time as possible according to what you can afford. Lenders often give better rates if you borrow larger amounts or pay back over a longer period. Yet taking more time to pay off the loan may not be the best option. If you lose your job or face other financial pressures, a long-term debt will be an additional burden. Equally, if you are suddenly able to pay off the loan early, you may be charged a penalty of some of the interest on a long-term loan.

Secured loans

Secured borrowing includes mortgages or other loans that are linked to your house or another major asset. The money you borrow is literally secured against the value of the property you own. Put simply, this means that if you fail to repay the secured loan (or your mortgage), your home can be taken from you and sold to cover your debts, even if they are significantly smaller than the property's value. Of course, this type of loan is only available if you have property or a major asset against which it can be secured. As with any loan, it is crucial to borrow only what you can afford to pay back.

Q. What is a secured loan?

A. This is when you borrow money and sign a document to say that the property you own can be sold if you fail to repay the debt.

Extending your mortgage

If you already have a mortgage, it may be cheaper to add to the cost of your mortgage rather than taking out a separate secured loan.

Rising property prices may be bad news for first-time buyers, but for existing homeowners this can provide the opportunity to reap rewards. If your home has gone up in value since you bought it, the difference between the amount you still owe on your mortgage and the amount your house is now worth is known as 'equity' and represents an increase on your investment. If you want to make this money work for you, you can extend your mortgage and withdraw some of the cash. In the UK, this effectively means you are borrowing at a rate of around 5 per cent instead of the 10 to 20 per cent through loans or credit cards.

If you want to release the money, you need to remortgage the property to bring your mortgage into line with the amount of equity you want to borrow. However, withdrawing some or all of the positive equity in your home brings its own set of problems. The temptation to over-borrow is very real, and while many homeowners use the cash to reinvest in their homes through improvements or extensions, there is nothing to stop the money being spent on one-off purchases such as holidays or cars. It is essential to consider whether you can afford the higher or extra repayments that your revised mortgage will bring.

The risk of a secured loan is weighted against you, and so this is often the cheapest way to borrow. Nonetheless, take into consideration any costs associated with changing or increasing your mortgage to borrow more – it is crucial that you don't overstretch yourself or your mortgage.

Problems can also arise if the housing market enjoys a buoyant period leading homeowners to believe that their good fortune will continue. If the market drops and stays low, those who have withdrawn much or all of the equity from their homes could end up with no additional value in their property or, worse still, negative equity. This is where the mortgage is higher than the value of the property. In their excitement at the prospect of a windfall, many homeowners overlook the need to increase their life insurance to cover the new, extended mortgage – another cost to remember.

Read paperwork carefully so that you know the level of risk. This is particularly important if you are thinking of taking out a secured loan to pay off several unsecured loans, for instance, if you are extending your mortgage to pay off credit card and overdraft debts.

Overdrafts

An overdraft can be attached to your bank account and provide flexibility for your cash flow by giving you access to an agreed amount of money if you need it. For instance, if your bank grants you a £1,000 overdraft, it could be useful if you have a cheque that is clearing just before pay day. But overdrafts should only be used on a temporary basis when you really need them. You should not use them as a day-to-day extension of your bank account.

Of course, overdrafts are a form of borrowing and so you have to pay for them. If you are £1,000 overdrawn every month for a year with a typical high street bank, it is likely to cost around £180 per year. Online banks may charge considerably less – around £80 per year.

Most bank accounts will not let you make cash withdrawals if your account is empty but they may honour cheques that take you beyond your bank balance into an unauthorized overdraft. If this happens, you will be charged a much higher rate of interest – possibly double the usual overdraft rate – and perhaps a fee on top. The bank will probably write you a letter, pointing out the unauthorized borrowing, and will impose an admin charge of around £25 for the cost of sending it. The fees and charges may come out of your already overdrawn account straight away, putting you even deeper into the red. So if you think you're about to go unexpectedly overdrawn, call the bank. It's more likely to be sympathetic if you give some warning.

MYTH: My bank loves me – it keeps increasing my overdraft so I must be doing okay with my money.

FACT: Your bank sees you as a way to make profits. It knows you will max the overdraft and it wants to put temptation in your way. Learn to say no.

Loan sharks

Borrowing money is something that most of us do at some stage in our lives. What do you do if your bank has turned you down for a loan and you still need to borrow money? You are not alone. That is the position of an estimated 7 million people in Britain who are on low incomes, have poor credit records or both, and are at the mercy of unscrupulous lenders.

Credit providers want to lend you as much money or give you as much credit as they can. Consequently if you can't get a loan from a respectable source, such as a bank or building society, there must be a good reason for it. It's probably because your present income and debt would cause you real problems in repaying any new loan. This may be hard for you to accept, but it's better to accept this than to get involved with an unlicensed lender.

How the loan gets out of control

While many moneylenders may be perfectly fair and honest, unfortunately some are not. These unlicensed lenders are known as 'loan sharks' and you should avoid them at all costs. Loan sharks will lend you money even when everybody else has turned you down, but they will also charge you very high rates of interest. Mainstream banks and other lenders typically charge interest rates of between 5 per cent and 17 per cent a year in the UK while the loan sharks charge as much as 1000 per cent. This means that if you borrow £500 at this rate, it will cost you an incredible £5,000 in interest over a year – money that you will owe to the lender and have to repay. You will almost certainly have to pay interest on that interest, too, making your debt grow higher. Yet desperate borrowers do sign up because they fail to understand the figures or choose not to think about it.

If you struggle to repay the loan – and the chances of this are high – the next thing you know is that you're taking out another loan to repay the first one. Then, perhaps you'll take out another loan to repay the second loan, and you just keep getting deeper and deeper into debt.

If you cannot repay what you owe

If you start to miss payments or fall short on payments you are likely to find that the nice, helpful moneylender will turn nasty. He or she may physically threaten you or your family. They may also demand any social security benefit book you may have. All of this is against the law, as is threatening you by letters or phone calls. If you find yourself in this position, you should complain to the police. The Trading Standards service may also be able to help you (see Part 5).

Alternatives

There are some properly regulated mainstream lenders who will lend to people on low incomes or with bad credit histories. In fact some firms specialize in lending to people with a poor credit rating. You can also check to see if there are any Credit Unions established in your area. Credit Unions are owned and controlled by their members who pool savings to offer loans to members at low rates of interest. Each Credit Union has a 'common bond' that determines who can join it. The common bond may be people living or working in the same area, people working for the same employer, or people belonging to the same association such as a church or trade union. Credit Unions are also known as 'people's banks' and are growing in popularity among those who have been refused credit elsewhere.

7

Support available now

Being in debt can be a lonely and frightening experience, but you don't need to cope with it alone. The good news is that there is plenty of help and advice available and it costs nothing. There are several national organizations in the UK that provide counselling, advice or just a friendly ear if you have concerns about money. Here is a guide to who they are and what they do. Their details are also given in Part 5, Chapter 18.

The Citizens Advice Bureaux

The service the Citizens Advice Bureaux provides helps people to resolve their legal, money and other problems by providing free information and advice from over 3,200 locations in the UK, and by influencing policymakers. Citizens Advice and each Citizens Advice Bureau are registered charities reliant on over 20,000 volunteers. The majority of their advisers are trained volunteers, helping people to resolve over 5.6 million problems every year. Before seeing an adviser about debt, Citizens Advice recommends that you gather together all your financial papers. These should include any court papers and letters, bills and credit agreements, and details of your income and expenditure and that of your spouse or partner.

If you have to wait for an appointment with an adviser, it may be useful to tell creditors that you have contacted an adviser for help. Most creditors welcome the involvement of a specialist adviser. They may be willing to hold off action to enable an agreement to be reached. See Part 5 for contact details.

The Consumer Credit Counselling Service (CCCS)

The CCCS is a registered charity whose purpose is to assist people in financial difficulty by providing free, independent, impartial and realistic advice. You can speak with a freephone helpline counsellor who performs an immediate assessment of the situation resulting in the offer of emergency help, self-help material or a counselling interview. The interview can take place over the phone or face to face in one of the centres, and CCCS will send you information to read in advance. The interview involves a full review of the credit and debt situation followed by a recommendation.

The first priority, wherever possible, is to allow fully for your essential expenditure, priority debts and living expenses. Then the counsellor will assess whether you have enough left over to make an offer of repayment to other creditors. If you do, the CCCS asks creditors to freeze interest, stop penalties, accept a longer repayment period and sometimes a reduced sum. Many creditors now have such respect for the CCCS that they accept its repayment proposals without further checks. See Part 5 for contact details.

National Debtline

This is a telephone helpline for people with debt problems in England, Wales and Scotland. The service is free, confidential and independent. The organization is committed to discussing your debt problems and the options available to you. The specialist advice given over the telephone is backed up with written self-help materials which are sent out to you for free. In certain circumstances, the organization can assist in setting up a free debt management plan for you. See Part 5 for contact details.

> **MYTH:** *Everyone I know is in debt so it must be a way of life.*
>
> **FACT:** It doesn't have to be. Life without debt gives you freedom and peace of mind. Thousands of people live life without going into debt.

Payplan

Payplan is one of the UK's leading debt management companies, assisting individuals who have unmanageable debts and working closely with charities such as National Debtline. Unlike most debt management companies, Payplan provides a free debt management service and is an independent company whose aim is to help people set up and keep to a manageable repayment plan. Its services are paid for by the UK credit industry which believes people should have access to free help with their debt problems.

First, Payplan will carry out a full assessment of your financial situation. They will then approach your creditors and ask them to approve the offer of reduced payments. You then make one monthly payment to Payplan and they send the (pro-rata) amounts directly to your creditors (usually by electronic bank transfer). All of this money directly reduces your debt.

Payplan will help and support you throughout the duration of your arrangement. You will be given an individual case officer who will be available to help you should you experience any problems. Case officers undertake regular reviews of your circumstances to ensure that your Payplan arrangement is still working. The arrangement continues until all of your debts are cleared. See Part 5 for contact details.

The Samaritans

The Samaritans provides confidential emotional support 24 hours a day for people who are experiencing feelings of distress or despair, including those that may lead to suicide. They are there for you if you're worried about something, feel upset or confused, or you just want to talk to someone. See Part 5 for contact details.

8

Bankruptcy and individual voluntary arrangements (IVAs)

Going bankrupt used to be a shameful thing and a last resort to be avoided at all costs. Since a number of UK laws were changed in 2004, it has become easier to go bankrupt, and more and more people have been choosing to do this after failing to cope with their debts.

Bankruptcy proceedings free you from overwhelming debts so you can make a fresh start – subject to some restrictions – and make sure your assets are shared out fairly among your creditors.

Anyone can go bankrupt but, despite the relaxation of rules and increased appeal, it is by no means an easy option and you should not consider it without understanding how it will affect you in the short and long term.

How bankruptcy works

A UK court will make a bankruptcy order after a petition has been presented by you or by one or more creditors who are owed by you at least £750 in unsecured debt. A bankruptcy order can still be made even if you refuse to acknowledge the proceedings or refuse to agree to them. You should therefore co-operate fully once the bankruptcy proceedings have begun. If you dispute the creditor's claim, you should try to reach a settlement before the bankruptcy petition is due to be heard as this can be difficult and expensive to address after the event. The bankruptcy order is advertised in *The London Gazette*, an official UK publication that contains legal notices, and in a local or national newspaper or both.

Once a bankruptcy order has been made, you must comply with a number of requests from the Official Receiver (OR). These include providing documentation and a full list of assets. You must stop using your bank, building society, credit card and similar accounts straightaway and you cannot obtain new accounts or credit of £500 or more from any person without first disclosing the fact that you are bankrupt. You may also have to go to court to explain why you are in debt. If you do not co-operate, you could be arrested.

How bankruptcy affects you

If you are made bankrupt, you will no longer control your assets, including the contents of your home. The OR will decide whether the value of your possessions is more than the cost of a reasonable replacement. Any assets seized will be disposed of by the OR or by an insolvency practitioner – appointed as trustee – to pay the fees, costs and expenses of the bankruptcy and then your creditors.

You may also be required to make contributions towards the bankruptcy debts from your income. This will be based on affordability and is kept under review. A trustee cannot usually claim a pension as an asset if your bankruptcy petition was presented on or after 29 May 2000, provided that the pension scheme has been approved by HM Revenue & Customs. However, they will be able to claim your life assurance policy.

If you own your home, whether freehold or leasehold, solely or jointly, mortgaged or otherwise, your interest in the home will form part of your estate which will be dealt with by your trustee. The home may have to be sold to go towards paying your debts. If your husband, wife or children are living with you, it may be possible for the sale to be put off until after the end of the first year of your bankruptcy to provide an opportunity for other housing arrangements to be made.

You will no longer have to make payments direct to creditors, although there are some exceptions, such as your mortgage lender. If you owe money to utilities suppliers, they may not chase the debts but could ask that you pay in advance for services or put the account in a partner's name. The OR will liaise directly with creditors to arrange any payments.

MYTH: I can go bankrupt if my debts get too much.

FACT: Bankruptcy is not a simple or easy option. It is a very serious position and has effects and restrictions on your finances and lifestyle that will last for years. It is not an easy way out.

What happens when you are discharged from bankruptcy

You are usually discharged from bankruptcy after 12 months, although this could take up to two years if your bankruptcy order mentions a certificate of summary administration. The court issues a certificate of summary administration where the unsecured debts are less than the small bankruptcy level (£20,000) and the debtor has not been previously adjudged bankrupt or made any financial arrangements with creditors within the last five years. Discharge releases you from most of the debts you owed at the date of the bankruptcy order, but exceptions include fines and debts arising from fraud. When you are discharged, you can borrow money or carry on business. You can act as a company director unless you are disqualified from doing so as a result of a separate order arising from your involvement with a company.

When you are discharged, there may still be assets that you owned during bankruptcy that the trustee has not yet dealt with such as your home, a pension, or an interest in a will or trust fund. These assets are still controlled by the trustee, who can deal with them at any time in the future.

This may not be until a number of years after your discharge. You must tell the OR about assets you obtain after the trustee has finished dealing with your case but before you are discharged as they could be claimed to pay your creditors.

With some assets – such as your home and some types of assurance policy – your spouse, a partner, a relative or friend may want to buy your interest. He or she should get in touch with the trustee straightaway to find out how much they would have to pay. Usually, you may keep all assets you acquire after your discharge.

Alternatives to bankruptcy

If you have exhausted all avenues in an attempt to resolve your debt problems, including taking advice from specialist counsellors (see Chapters 7 and 19), there are still alternatives to bankruptcy.

Administration orders

If one or more of your creditors has obtained a court judgement against you in the UK, the county court may make an administration order. This allows you to make regular payments to the court towards the money you owe your creditors. To qualify, your total debts must not be more than £5,000 and you will need enough regular income to make weekly or monthly repayments. There are no fees involved but the court will take a small percentage from the money you pay towards its costs. If you do not pay regularly, the order could be cancelled and you may become subject to the same restrictions as someone who is bankrupt.

Individual voluntary arrangements (IVAs)

A more formal version of the administration order is an IVA. This begins with a formal proposal to your creditors to pay part or all of your debts. You need to apply to the court and must be helped by an insolvency practitioner who will charge a fee. Any agreement reached with your creditors will be binding.

There is no maximum or minimum level of debt and no maximum or minimum level of repayments, except what is acceptable to your creditors. IVAs can work well if you have friends or relatives prepared to help pay or contribute towards paying your debts or if your income enables you to pay regular sums to creditors. IVAs also usually allow you to retain more control over your assets, including your home, and you can avoid the restrictions of bankruptcy.

As with bankruptcy, an IVA is not an easy option and you should think very carefully and seek expert advice before you sign up to one. This is particularly important if you have been attracted by one of the many television adverts for companies which make IVAs look quick and easy.

Don't fall for the adverts. An IVA can leave a big black mark on your credit record for a long time and it is likely to come with a large fee.

9

Becoming debt-free: a simple guide

The previous chapters in both Parts 1 and 2 have set out in detail everything you need to know and do to start paying off debts and to get a better grip on your money. There is plenty to take in, but don't panic. No one expects you to be a financial expert. Here is a reminder of the key stages you are working through.

Put together a budget

Keep your budget simple, with one column to list your incoming funds and another to detail your outgoing costs. Be honest and make sure that the amounts are realistic. Include everything from your mortgage and bills through to your travel, lunch and toiletry expenses. Try to spot areas where you can cut back or if you can do without non-essential items. It may mean that you have to reduce your social life for a while – be prepared to make sacrifices.

Prioritize your bills and debts

Make sure that your mortgage or rent and other essential household bills, such as electricity, council tax and gas, come top of the list. Then put credit card bills, loans and any other debts in order, with the highest interest payments first. If in doubt, look at the lists on pages 9–10.

Priority debts are debts owed to creditors who can take the strongest legal actions against you if you do not pay. It is not the size of the debt that makes it a priority, but what the creditors can do to recover their money. If you have:

- Mortgage or rent arrears, the lender or landlord can repossess your home or evict you

- Unpaid utilities debts, your electricity, gas or telephone can be disconnected

- Unpaid maintenance, child support, council tax or fines, a court can use bailiffs to repossess your goods. If, after this, you still have arrears unpaid, you can be sent to prison.

- Income tax or VAT debts, you can be made bankrupt or imprisoned for non-payment.

Hire purchase agreements on essential items, for instance where you buy a vehicle for work, are also priority debts. If you have any of these debts, you must deal with them before you offer to repay any of your non-priority debts.

Examples of non-priority debts are:

- Credit card and store card arrears

- Catalogue arrears

- Bank overdrafts and loans

- Benefits overpayments

- Hire purchase agreements for non-essential items, such as a television

- Money borrowed from family or friends.

You cannot be imprisoned for not paying non-priority debts. You are unlikely to lose your home or your essential goods. However, if you make no offers to pay, without explaining why, the creditors will take you to court. If you still fail to pay when the court has ordered it, the creditors can take further action. For example, they can get another court order allowing them to send bailiffs in.

Assess your situation

It may be scary but getting in touch and staying in touch with the people you owe money to is essential. Be brave and it will make all the difference. Consider asking lenders to reduce payments or freeze interest if it is clear from your budget that:

- You will be late making payments

- You do not have enough spare cash to start reducing your debt

• You cannot even keep up minimum payments.

Contact the creditors in writing or by telephone, explain the situation and let them know what you can pay – even the smallest payment will show that you are making an effort. If it has not already done so, the bank or card company may freeze your account until you have caught up with payments, but they may also freeze the interest you owe or permit reduced payments. Make sure you keep copies of letters and notes of telephone conversations. Some banks and building societies take people more seriously if they come through an advice centre such as the Citizens Advice Bureaux or similar organizations as it shows that you are serious about your finances. If you do negotiate lowered repayments, be aware that this could have an effect on your credit record (see Chapter 13).

MYTH: One more credit card won't make any difference – I already have three.

FACT: It depends how much you owe on the others and why you want the next one. The chances are it will lead to nothing but more debt. If you are honest, you will admit that you – and your credit rating – could do without it.

Consider specialist debt advice

Don't be afraid to ask for help. You will almost certainly find it helpful, particularly if:

- You are in a vicious circle, using one credit card to pay another

- Your overdraft is increasing every month

- You are using credit cards to buy essential food or withdraw cash on a regular basis.

Another signal that you need help is if you are in difficulty with 'priority' debts such as mortgage arrears or council tax. If you are on a very low income, and at least partly dependent on benefits, you may need specialist welfare or debt advice to see if you are claiming all the benefits to which you are entitled. You may find you are entitled to something you are not currently receiving.

A new industry has grown up over the last few years offering debt management in return for a fee. Don't rush to take up these offers as an easy way out. They represent an expensive way of resolving your debt problem and do not provide any services that you cannot secure on your own, free of charge. A free debt management service is available from Payplan, an independent UK organization funded by the credit industry. Get in touch with an organization such as the UK Consumer Credit Counselling Service (CCCS) or National Debtline for free information and advice. Contact details for all of the above can be found in Part 5.

Stay debt free

When you're debt-free, make a new budget and stick to it. Cut up any remaining credit cards unless you can pay balances in full each month. Better still, stick to a cash or a debit card that takes the money straight out of your current account when you pay. Managing your bank account online gives you more control and allows you to keep an eye on your spending – and saving. There are ideas, tips and further information on this in Parts 3, 4 and 5.

Emotional lifelines

Change is not easy. Becoming debt-free may feel unnatural and scary and you may want to stop what you are doing and go back to the familiarity and comfort of your old habits, however much anxiety they brought. Don't stop now. You have made so much progress by picking up this book, making sense of your situation and beginning to tackle your debt.

It was very hard to cut up my credit cards while I dealt with my debt and got back on track. Apart from not being able to spend on them, I was having to pay off the debt. The rewards became clear when my first couple of statements showed that my debt was getting smaller and not bigger for a change.

Nick

Making time

If you are working and looking after yourself and a family, it can be very hard to find the time to go through the paperwork and get in touch with creditors and the organizations that can help. Don't allow yourself to make lots of excuses for putting things off. Use a diary to record dates when payments are due and give yourself small incentives to reward each step you take – an inexpensive treat such as some favourite food or a trip to the cinema at the end of a hard week can work wonders. It is important that you are not too hard on yourself.

Sharing the burden

Now that you have begun to make progress, it should be a little easier to talk to your partner, a close friend or relative about your debt and to ask for their support as you deal with it. If you have not yet told them and feel nervous about opening up, there is more about this in Chapter 2 that may help.

If you have told those closest to you, now is the time to allow them to help and encourage you and to support you emotionally. Don't be afraid to ask for help. If you have the benefit of working through this as part of a team, then you cannot go wrong. Do remember to keep talking to those supporting you, particularly if their lifestyle is changing because there is less money around. If you have children and would prefer not to discuss the details with them, try to keep things as smooth as possible but perhaps explain that you have a difficult puzzle you are trying to work out and it may take some time. Tell them you need them to help by being patient with you. Even younger children can be surprisingly understanding at times.

Ongoing support

If you have visited your doctor and found that counselling is helping or if you are taking medication to help with depression or stress, it's important to follow the instructions your doctor and counsellor give you. As you begin to pay off the money you owe and make your life better, you will start feeling better, but resist any temptation to stop taking medication or end counselling against the advice of professionals. This could do more harm than good. Talk to your doctor or counsellor if you feel ready to end treatment.

Part 3:
Long-term
Challenges and
Future Hopes

10

Money matters

You have come so far already. Take some time to think about the progress you have made – it is no small thing and it will encourage you to keep going. Some of the steps you have completed will take more getting used to than others, but don't give up. You may not see instant, overnight results, but this does not mean you are not making progress. Every day you are spending less and paying off more. Cutting out unnecessary spending could mean a significant change in lifestyle which may be hard-going initially but once the benefits begin to show – more cash, more control and more choice – your efforts will be rewarded.

Take stock

If you have slipped a little on spending or debt then stay calm and review your budget. Work out how to get back on track. This could involve cutting back a little more this month or next. If you can already see savings, then resist the urge to spend them. Try not to feel overwhelmed.

- Keep en eye on the amount of debt being paid off – this will give you an ongoing sense of progress and achievement.

- Learn new habits that deliver the opposite sort of behaviour from debt-building, for example, open bills as soon as they arrive and know how to pay them.

- Begin to plan and build a healthier financial future with no debt.

Q. I sometimes take cash out using my credit card, does this cost me more?

A. Yes, with most cards you will pay at least one fee and a higher rate of interest on 'cash advances'. You are also likely to be charged interest on the cash straightaway. Avoid doing this unless it is an absolute emergency.

Get closer to your money

Now that opening your bills and statements is no longer scary, you can make good use of them. Knowing exactly what is happening to your money is the best way to keep it under control and to avoid slipping off your repayment plans or taking on more debt. Get into the habit of reading all your statements and bills carefully to check for errors. Keep receipts and cross-check them against the paperwork.

Check that any regular standing orders and direct debits attached to your bank account are shown properly on the statement. If you don't recognize any, make a note to follow them up with your bank. It could be that you are paying for forgotten memberships or subscriptions – you may have ignored regular transfers for small amounts, but they all add up.

MYTH: There is no such thing as a credit blacklist – it's a myth created to scare big spenders.

FACT: As you may soon find out, credit ratings are real, and if you get into debt and make late credit or loan repayments, you will become increasingly undesirable to lenders.

Online banking

If you have access to the internet, you may find it helpful to set up online access to your bank account. Some of the easiest ways to lose track of your day-to-day finances and cash flow include:

- Never checking your balance

- Forgetting that cheques or direct debits are about to leave your account

- Failing to read statements.

Banking online can help to avoid these problems.

Most banks and building societies will give you instructions and help you to bank online without charge. Once you have set up passwords – which you must keep safe – you can access your account 24 hours a day. In addition to keeping close tabs on your balance and being able to spot errors more quickly, you can pay bills, transfer cash and carry out many of the banking activities you normally arrange in a branch, including applying for savings accounts, loans and credit cards online. Bear in mind that some online banks update information in real time, while others do it once a day. Many online banks highlight imminent outgoing amounts from cheques, standing orders or direct debits so that you don't get carried away by thinking your balance is larger than you expected.

Talk to your bank and start managing your account online. You will still have access to your account through branches and you won't have to give up your passbooks or cheque books, you will simply have an extra way of keeping an eye on your money. Setting up your account online may take a few days to complete but start today and you will be surprised how quickly you get the hang of it. If you don't have a computer at home, your online access can still be useful at work or through library computers.

Banks have a priority to make their customers feel comfortable about online banking, and they take great steps to maintain a high level of security. In fact, the only really vulnerable area is your PIN (personal identification number) and password. That is why it is so important to keep them safe. Provided you keep your password confidential and ensure that others can't see your computer screen when you sign on, internet banking is just as safe as any other form of banking. Take simple precautions such as clearing your internet browser's cache when you exit (use the Tools menu, Internet Options and General tab and delete the Temporary Internet files to do this). If your browser has the ability to remember passwords and user names, consider disabling this function or always decline the option to save your bank password. If you access your account on a public computer, close the internet browser after use. Ask a friend or even your librarian to assist if you are not sure.

Keep your budget under review

You don't have to wait for any major changes in your circumstances to justify a budget review. Now you have done your budget once, it should be very easy to dust it off and check your progress as often as you like. To begin with, you may want to review it once a month because there is so much going on. If you have considerable debts and are paying them off, this is another good way to keep an eye on everything. You don't need to become obsessive about it but once you have control over your finances, it makes sense to maintain this. A budget review will give you a clear idea of what your money is doing all the time and it will mean no more nasty surprises.

11

Look at your spending habits

Becoming debt-free is a big step. Staying debt-free is just as important. You probably had to make changes to your lifestyle to pay off your debt. More changes can help you to make the most of your income and break any bad spending habits.

Try to think carefully about purchases and ask yourself 'Is this absolutely necessary?' Consider how several small, short-term purchases can be sacrificed for more substantial or longer-term goals. For example, spending £1.50 on a coffee every working day will cost you around £400 a year. You don't need to live like a hermit, but be aware of the options you have when you save as well as spend.

Ask yourself the following questions:

- Are you buying lunch from a sandwich bar every day because you can never seem to organize packed lunches?
- Do you shop for clothes and accessories when you are bored?
- Are you 'habit' buying (e.g. buying a magazine as part of your routine while you wait for the train home) to distract yourself from a less exciting task or goal?
- Do you spend more because time always seems short and you need the quickest option, regardless of cost?
- Does your cash trickle away, leaving you broke before the end of the month?

If you answered yes to any of the above, you could change your spending habits for the better.

Your bank statements may show patterns of spending that you want to change. For example, if you binge-spend just after pay day, then always run out of cash long before the next pay day, aim to cut back and set a weekly spending limit.

Cut back and save

- Go through the lists of everyday spending and occasional costs and ask yourself: 'Is this absolutely necessary?'
- Can several small, short-term purchases be sacrificed for more substantial or longer-term goals?
- Tick the boxes below if you regularly buy any of the items listed. Then see how much you can save.

Item	Average cost	Monthly cost	How much you could save per year	
CD	£9.99 a week	£40.00	£480.00	❑
Coffee	£1.50 each working day	£30.00	£330.00	❑
Lip gloss	£8.99 a month	£8.99	£108.00	❑
Shoes	£80 every month	£80.00	£960.00	❑
Gym	£40 a month	£40	£480.00	❑

Total potential saving _____

Look for ways to reduce regular spending as well as splurges. The supermarket provides a classic opportunity to spend more than you planned, and these stores are designed to seduce you with items you did not plan to buy and to make you feel good about doing it. Beat the system by drawing up a shopping list before you go. Be single-minded and never go food shopping when you are hungry. Planning the food and meals you need for the week can also save you shopping time. If you spot three-for-one offers, think twice before grabbing them. They may be a false economy if the items go off before you can use them or if you end up buying things you don't need just because they were a 'bargain'.

Try not to head to shopping centres for browsing. Make sure that any shopping trip fits in with your budget and has a clear agenda. Put less time on your parking ticket if you want to limit your risk of a spending spree.

Many things that we buy are not essential. Sometimes, they are not even necessary – they may be lazy or indulgent purchases. We all do it, often because it is quicker or easier. To help you think twice before you spend, there are several key questions you can ask yourself:

- **If I had to draw out the cash to buy this, would I be so keen to have it?**

  Parting with cash is much harder than entering your PIN into a credit card machine. Don't let credit lull you into a false sense of riches.

- **Does this actually suit me or am I buying it because it is in the sale?**

  Finding a bargain is exciting but only if it is something you really want or need.

- **If I saw this item with a less attractive brand on the label, would it still appeal?**

  Whether it is an electrical gadget or a new dress, don't be seduced into paying more for the name on an item that otherwise might not be your cup of tea.

- **Is there an own-brand version of this available for less?**

  This applies everywhere from supermarket to boutique. Own brands are usually every bit as good as their more expensive counterparts. If in doubt, ask an assistant for advice on a specific item.

- **Once I pay the interest on my credit card, how much will this really cost me?**

If you don't completely clear your credit card balance every month, you can add up to 20 per cent onto the cost of your item.

- **This may be on special offer, but is it even worth the reduced amount?**

When is a bargain not a bargain? When you're really only buying it because you think you are getting it for less.

- **Even though this is buy one, get one free, do I really use it?**

It's hard to resist a give-away, but if you don't use hair mousse then you're not likely to start.

- **If I buy this, will it mean I cannot afford other things?**

It's one thing to splash out on something you

see, but will spending that money reduce your options on other purchases or activities later in the month?

Spot spending triggers

Using your budget and your bank and credit card statements, see if you can find any patterns:

- If you tend to spend lots of cash either on or just after pay day, you see your newly replenished bank balance as a bottomless pit. Banking online will help you keep a closer eye on your balance as it shrinks throughout the month.

- To avoid temptation, set up a monthly transfer to half your disposable income so that it disappears to a savings account before you can spend it.

- Transferring funds back to your current account when and if you need them can be done instantly online, but aim to set a target for the amount of disposable income you spend each month and spend within that amount.

Stop relying on credit

Paying off part of your credit card balance only to run it up to the limit again in the same month means you are 'robbing Peter to pay Paul'. In other words, you are spending money you cannot really afford, and being charged interest on it, month in and month out. You are not making any progress in getting your finances straight. Time to break the cycle.

It's a mistake to look upon any spare credit as part of your available funds when it is actually debt. Avoid relying on and using credit. Try leaving your credit card at home when you go shopping or when you might be tempted to splurge, such as immediately after you have paid part or all of your card bill. If being without your card makes you anxious in case you need it in an emergency, put some cash in an unused part of your wallet or purse so you know you have some extra if you really need it. This will only work if you keep the money for emergencies only. Buying a new CD or another pint is not an emergency, no matter how bad your day has been.

Q. I have been sent credit card cheques. Can I use these like a normal cheque book?

A. Although they look like bank account cheque books, these are just another way to spend your credit limit and get into debt. The cheques come with lots of fees and charges, and a higher interest rate than your card. Rip them up and call the card issuer to ask them not to send any more. These cheques are usually sent without you asking for them, and if they go astray in the post, they could end up in the hands of fraudsters.

If you view any spare credit as part of your available funds, it is time to rethink your spending. Look for opportunities to avoid using your flexible friend. These might include:

- Leaving your credit card at home when you go shopping or when you might be tempted to splash out.

- Not setting up a tab if you buy a round at the bar and choose to pay by credit card. A tab will encourage you to run up a bigger bill, particularly as the evening goes on and drinking may make you feel generous.

- Taking enough cash to pay for what you actually need to buy and leaving your cards at home when you go to the supermarket so that you are not tempted to fill up your trolley 'because it is all going on the card, so it doesn't matter'.

Get tough with yourself and don't undo all the great efforts you have made to become debt-free.

Struggling?

If you absolutely have to use your credit card, for instance, if you are paying for food with it, then aim to spend less and to use it less each month. Think twice before you spend. Ask yourself: 'If I had to draw out the cash to buy this, would I be so keen to have it?' Parting with cash is much harder than entering your PIN into a credit card machine. Don't let credit lull you into a false sense of riches. If you are not clearing your credit card balance every month, then once you pay the interest on your credit card, how much does a purchase really cost?

Avoid store cards

The worst type of plastic, UK store cards usually have interest rates of around 29 per cent or more. That's 10 per cent more than the most expensive credit card. If you spend £500 on a typical store card charging 29.9 per cent Annual Percentage Rate (APR) and pay it off in 12 months, you would pay £149.50 in interest. However, spend the same amount on a credit card with 10 months' interest-free credit for purchases, and you would only pay £24.91 in interest over the year – a saving of £124.59.

Store cardholders are often tempted by benefits such as loyalty schemes, discounts, special preview evenings and early access to sale stock. These benefits are easily outweighed by the high interest rates. It's best to avoid store cards completely – just say no every time you are asked, however persistent the salesperson is. The sales staff are often on targets and commission to get people to sign up – don't feel flattered if they ask you to apply.

> *MYTH: Store cards are cheaper than credit cards.*
>
> **FACT:** It's usually the opposite. It is possible to find credit cards that charge interest of around 6 per cent (i.e. you pay £6 for every £100 not paid off each month). But store cards tend to charge interest rates closer to 29 per cent.

Some people like to have an unused credit card for emergencies. This is only suitable if you can be absolutely sure that you will not be tempted to abuse it. A weekend in Paris or a new outfit does not constitute an emergency. Keep the '999' credit card in a secure place, but review what it offers you at least once a year. This will ensure that if you do need to use it, you are getting the best deal. Don't be put off by figures and small print on credit card adverts and contracts, and never be afraid to ask if you are not sure what something means. You won't be the first – or last – person to ask.

Nought per cent balance transfers – the catches

One of the easiest ways to make an impact on your credit card debt is to cut out the interest.

There are dozens of cards available that allow you to transfer your balance to a 0 per cent interest rate for an introductory period or to a very low rate for the life of the balance. Yet there may be some hidden catches. Providers offering the longest 0 per cent rate may boost their profits by putting a high interest rate on the card if you use it for purchases.

If you use the same card to pay off a balance and make purchases you can face problems. Repayments you make on the card will often be used by the issuer to pay off a certain part of your debt first, usually the transferred balance. This means that the cost of any purchases made will remain on the card as debt and will be charged at the purchase interest rate, which could be something like 19 per cent. You can overcome this by transferring a balance to one card and using another for purchases, making sure you get the best deal on each.

Pay close attention to any one-off fees that must be made for a balance transfer. These are usually between 1 per cent and 3 per cent of the amount transferred, so shop around.

Q. What's a balance transfer?

A. This involves taking out a new credit card and transferring the money you owe on a previous card to the new card. It is usually done to pay less interest on a credit card debt. However, although it may provide a breathing space, it is not a long-term solution because it just moves the debt around.

Get used to cash

The idea of getting through life for even a day without your credit cards may fill you with dread, but imagine trying it for a week. Get used to paying for things with cash again and it will remind you of the value of the items you buy and it will make you think twice about your spending habits. It is so much easier to hand over a plastic card than cash when you buy something, particularly if you know you cannot really afford it. This is particularly relevant with high-street spending where you can pretend to yourself that £50 here or there may not make a huge difference. In reality, if you had to hand over five £10 notes you might feel very differently about the purchase. Many of us rely on plastic, but it is easier to keep stretching finances when you do not have to think beyond your four-digit PIN number.

Go credit cold-turkey. Use your budget (see page 12) to work out your disposable income and to calculate how much cash you need to withdraw for each day or, better still, a whole week. Leave your credit cards at home – all of them – and brave the world of reality. If you normally use a debit card, avoid paying with it and stick to cash. At the end of the week, think about how many times you decided not to buy something because spending cash rather than using plastic made the item seem less appealing. Did you have less fun and less freedom using cash or did it feel more liberating and give you a sense of control?

Look closely at your cash

- Look for patterns in your bank accounts of cash withdrawals. Do you take what you need whenever you need it or do you draw out a limited amount each week? Now that you have a clear idea of your monthly disposable income, it should be easier to work out a weekly limit for cash withdrawals so that you curb any overspending.

- Another reason for avoiding lots of small, irregular cash withdrawals is that they make it harder to keep track of what's left in your account.

- Sticking to your limit and monitoring your account online will help you keep your finances steady throughout each month. There's nothing worse than running out of cash a week before pay day. This will usually mean you have to rely on credit so plan ahead to avoid the miserable run-up to getting paid again.

Use debit instead of credit

They may not have been around for as long as credit cards but debit cards work in quite a different way. Instead of building up a monthly bill, the things you buy using your debit card will be paid for with money that comes straight from your current account. This means that when you use your debit card to pay for things, you will need to think very carefully about whether you can really afford them. Using debit can help you avoid a 'buy now, pay later' attitude because you pay as soon as you buy.

If you do not already have a debit card or if you have one with limited use, such as Solo, then consider talking to your bank. If you are struggling to keep your current account in credit, then your bank may want to see an improvement in your money management before they issue a Maestro card.

Online banking can be helpful here – you can keep a close eye on the money leaving your account. Don't forget that some transactions take several days to come through your account so check carefully to ensure you are spending within your means.

Plan ahead

When you set yourself a budget for the week or month, it is easy to forget about occasional costs that may only come up once or twice a year but still have to be paid for. Think about:

- Holidays

- Birthdays

- Christmas

- Hen or stag parties or trips

- Weddings

- Christenings

- Home improvements such as decorating, furniture or gardening

- Dentist visits

- Optician visits and costs of glasses, contact lenses and accessories.

Some of these items may be hard to anticipate. Occasional spending may involve more pressure than other areas. Going to a wedding, for example, is not always easy to predict and can involve everything from the cost of a gift to extensive travel, cash for drinks and an overnight stay. It is also possible to spend a small fortune on hen and stag parties or trips – they can involve a budget covering anything from a night in the pub to a week abroad and everything in between.

Avoid the pressure

It is incredibly hard to own up to being broke or to miss out on an event or trip that is talked about for years after. However, if you're honest about your limited budget, you might find that others are relieved too. Big groups heading on big trips require excellent planning skills, and thinking ahead can help avoid unnecessary costs. Likewise, if you feel under pressure to buy expensive gifts for birthdays, weddings or leaving parties, talk to friends about perhaps setting a limit or clubbing together. You will probably find that they are relieved too.

To avoid nasty surprises when it comes to occasional spending, estimate some basic costs across the year and then total these to get an average yearly figure. Break down the amount to calculate the monthly sub-total for occasional spending. Remember, it is better to have some flexibility built into your budget than to be caught out.

Christmas

Of all the things that send people into over-borrowing and debt, Christmas has to be one of the biggest. Not only is debt as far from the real meaning of Christmas as is possible, but it is never an unexpected event. It happens on the same day every single year and yet seems to catch millions of people out. This is why loan companies, credit and store cards increase their advertising and special offers just before and after Christmas, when the bills start to arrive.

If you have spent so much in cash and credit that Christmas has left you well and truly in the red, you are not alone. In the UK, more than £1 trillion is owed in debt, meaning that an average of £17,000 is owed by every man, woman and child on mortgages, personal loans, overdrafts and credit cards. For many people, this represents a year's salary – imagine working for a whole year and paying every penny to credit card and mortgage lenders.

Malcolm Hurlston, chairman of the UK Consumer Credit Counselling Service (CCCS), advises that:

This record level of consumer credit is a timely reminder to take stock and ensure that credit hasn't run away with you. There are a trillion reasons to stop and think. Remember it's not how much you owe, but how much you owe relative to your income that's important. No-one should be spending more than a fifth of their monthly take-home pay on meeting minimum repayments on unsecured credit. If they are, they need to cut back.

Unfortunately, this sound advice may be too late for many. The average household in the UK borrows 140 per cent more than its combined income, and around 6 million families are said to be struggling to make credit repayments. So how can you get your own house in order and stop the tide of post-festive debt? Hurlston says that the simplest way of doing this is to stop paying for things by credit card until the existing balances have been substantially reduced. That way you will avoid becoming over-indebted.

Instead of hiding from the bills, make a New Year's resolution to tackle your debts head on, and ensure that the same thing does not happen again next year. If you find yourself struggling, don't be afraid to seek help.

Ninety-five per cent of people will probably be OK but for those who are worried, it is best to seek help as soon as possible. Over half of our clients say they waited too long – over a year after they knew they had a problem – before seeking help.

Malcolm Hurlston

The hangover we get from Christmas is mainly caused by a lack of planning. Start making notes early in the year about who you want to buy presents for. Don't be afraid to make changes to long-established family 'traditions', especially if they involve gifts for dozens of relatives you rarely see. Begin by cutting out grown-ups and buying just for children. Suggest that everyone spends no more than a certain amount, say £5 or £10. Think about the extra costs of food, decorations and travel, and use your budget to guide you to what you can afford rather than what you think you must have or what others expect. Managing the expectations of others well in advance should mean that you can have a stress-free and debt-free festive season.

Maximize your income

If you are not able to take on extra work to increase your income, it is worth spending some time looking at your bills and trying to reduce them in order to make your existing income go further.

Your mortgage

Your biggest monthly bill is your mortgage, so it makes sense to ensure that this is as low as possible. More than a quarter of homeowners are paying their lender's standard variable rate (SVR) on their mortgage. This type of rate goes up or down as the lender adjusts it to economic and market conditions. It is usually the most uncompetitive and expensive rate to be on and the way it moves up and down will not suit those who want to pay a set amount every month. If you are paying this type of rate, you can almost certainly save money by switching your mortgage. You don't have to switch to a new mortgage lender unless you want to. You should find that your existing mortgage lender can offer you a cheaper rate.

Almost a third of homeowners are put off switching their mortgage because they think it takes a lot of time and hassle. A similar number think it would be expensive to switch. Some homeowners don't know where to start, others believe they can only remortgage if they are moving home. These misconceptions are costing homeowners a fortune.

How to review and switch your mortgage

1 Decide what you want to get out of your mortgage review – do you want lower monthly payments, the security of a fixed rate, flexibility, debt consolidation or a mixture of these?

2 Check your existing mortgage – what's your current rate? How much do you pay each month? Are you tied into any fixed-rate or discounted deal, if so, for how long? Check you are not going to be subject to a penalty.

3 Get a redemption statement – ask your current lender for a written redemption statement. This shows the exact outstanding balance of your loan, the remaining term and any fees or penalties you'll be charged for redeeming your mortgage.

4 Shop around among other lenders for a better deal. It's advisable to collect and compare information from at least five lenders or you can get an independent broker to scour the market for you. When comparing the savings you would make on different deals, look behind the headline rate and monthly payments on offer. Ask for details of the up-front costs and if the deal means paying for any compulsory insurance.

5 Decide if you want to stay with your existing lender - once you have gathered the information, you will be in a strong position to negotiate. Some lenders do not make re-mortgaging easy for their own customers. Many don't offer the best deals to customers who want to remortgage rather than move house. Don't be put off. Sometimes when customers threaten to take their business elsewhere, lenders relent and reveal their best 'under the counter' deals.

6 Gather together your paperwork – depending on whether you stay with your existing lender or move lenders, you will need proof of ID, residence and income. You will also be asked for one year's mortgage statement, between

one and three months' payslips and bank statements, a P60 certificate of pay and tax deducted, and sometimes an employer's reference. Being prepared means you can start saving as soon as possible.

Your gas and electricity bills

Since 1996 when the gas and electricity markets opened up, energy companies have been competing to undercut each other and offer better deals to customers. You could cut your bills by switching one or both providers.

Energy regulator Ofgem says the biggest gain is for customers who have never switched. It believes they could save around £100 on their annual home energy bill and perhaps more if they change the way they pay. The reason is that if you have never moved supplier, you are probably still getting your energy from what was once a monopoly and being are charged their highest tariff.

Switching energy companies is easy to do. If you have access to the internet at home or through your local library then make use of the free, impartial comparison websites that are accredited by Energywatch, such as

SwitchwithWhich, uSwitch and MoneyExpert. It will only take a few minutes of your time. If you decide to make the switch after your energy comparison, you will need to fill in some personal details, which will be passed straight on to your new supplier. The switching process usually takes around 28-45 days. Some suppliers offer combined plans to customers who choose to have both their gas and electricity supplied by a single company. These plans are often referred to as 'dual fuel' deals, and typically include incentives and reduced prices.

Consumer campaigners Which? suggest the following ways to save money on your utility bills:

- Pay by direct debit – all companies should give you a discount for doing this.

- Using the same supplier for gas and electricity may also save you cash – check out dual fuel tariffs.

- Be more energy efficient – contact the Energy Savings Trust or call your energy supplier and ask them for advice on how to be more energy efficient, thus cutting your bills.

Your phone bills

There are now around 200 licensed phone companies in the UK, each offering different tariffs and packages according to the types of phone calls they provide, such as local, national and international calls. Some of these phone companies are household names such as BT, while others are less well known. What this means for you is a world of competitive offers therefore big savings to be made on your bills.

Think about how and when you use your phone most. If you regularly make international calls, some providers specialize in cheaper overseas tariffs. Others may offer cheaper rates if you make most of your calls at evenings or weekends.

It is now easier than ever to shop around, using a free home telephone comparison service such as the one offered by uSwitch.com. The online services will ask you questions about your telephone usage, then will search hundreds of tariffs to provide a list of options based on your requirements, which could save you money. Once you have selected a new telephone company, they can even arrange the switch for you. If you do not have access to the internet, you can contact uSwitch on 0845 601 2856.

For your mobile phone, you may want to consider pre-pay tariffs, where you buy the phone and top up the credit. This is ideal if you want a mobile only for emergencies or to receive calls. These are also handy for people who want to manage their call costs. As a rule of thumb, Which? recommends that if your bill is more than £15 a month and you use your phone for more than three minutes a day, you might save money with a contract.

Emotional lifelines

At this stage, you should not be afraid to keep asking for help and support from both your loved ones and your creditors. You will need this support as your new budget, repayments schedule and changes in your lifestyle take effect.

Make sure you are not too hard on yourself – it is important to try to cope with any guilt and stress, particularly if loved ones are affected by budget and lifestyle constrictions as a result of the debt. Consider setting up small rewards for you and for those helping you to keep you going and to give you something to look forward to.

Try to spot the signs that you may be slipping back into old habits. For example, you might find it is much easier to reach for a credit card if you are in a hurry. Making time is not easy but it will help you stick to your plan. If you do feel you are losing control a little, tell your loved ones so that they can help you spot and avoid any bad habits.

12

Debt and relationships

The end of a relationship is painful enough but once the hearts and flowers have disappeared, the last thing you want to deal with is debts and bills. Half of all marriages in the UK now end in divorce – and that means financial misery for many. There are ways to minimize the financial hurt, but because two cannot live as cheaply as one, separating your financial relationship simply and quickly should be a priority.

Joint credit

It is easy to take the plunge and share a bank account or loan with your loved one, especially if you are married or live together. However, many people do not realize that joint credit can be risky. One partner's finances can have a big effect on the other's.

If you take out a loan or credit card in both your names, perhaps to pay for new furniture or a holiday, you will be jointly *and* individually liable for the money that you owe. This means that if your partner leaves you and refuses to pay their share, the bank or finance company can and will come after you for the whole debt, not just your share of it. This is what you agree to when you sign up to joint credit. Even if you trust your partner completely, you must still be prepared to pay 100 per cent of the money back if the worst happens.

Joint credit may be tempting, especially if you are offered more credit as a couple or if one of you has a poor credit record. Yet you should always avoid the temptation to borrow more than you can afford. This applies to any credit agreements, loans, overdrafts, rent arrears on joint tenancies, arrears on joint mortgages, council tax payments and water charges on properties that have been jointly occupied. The key point is whether or not you signed a joint agreement. Generally speaking, you are not liable for your partner's, or anyone else's debts, unless you signed an agreement or acted as guarantor. In the UK, the two main exceptions to this are council tax and water charges. It is worth noting that regardless of the terms of your divorce settlement, creditors will still pursue you both for outstanding debts in both your names, even if one of you agrees in writing to pay them off.

Chapter 13 also explains how your partner's bad money habits can have a lasting impact on your own credit record.

Joint accounts

Your joint account might have seemed like a caring, sharing move to make, but if you reach the stage where you cannot trust your partner then it could cause you regrets. Limitless, single-signature withdrawals mean that the account could be drained by either one of you, leaving the other with a nasty shock. Worse still, if one partner goes overdrawn on the account, both of you are liable for the debt.

> **MYTH:** *The bank is chasing me for a loan on our joint account but my partner spent the money so I don't need to repay it.*
>
> **FACT:** If you sign up to joint credit, you are legally responsible for the repayments jointly with your partner and separately if they fail to pay.

It may not be romantic, but many couples opt for the 'three-pot' system for this reason. They keep their own individual accounts and have a joint account for the mortgage and shared bills. If your relationship breaks down, you can then close the joint account and advise your bank on how bills will be paid in the future. Separate savings accounts also give you each more control. In a modern age of internet banking, transfers can be made between accounts in a few seconds, when needed. If you decide to have joint accounts that then need closing, the bank or building society is not obliged to convert the joint account into a single one or to offer you a new account of your own if they feel that your financial position is not sound.

Joint mortgages

The biggest debt you agree to share with a partner is your mortgage. If you take it out jointly, you will be jointly liable for the debt. Talk to your lender as soon as you think there will be a change in financial circumstances. It is crucial to keep the lines of communication open with your lender so that they will view your circumstances sympathetically if you need their help. If you find that your partner is refusing to pay their share of the monthly mortgage payments and you are able to pay them on your own for a short period, make sure you keep evidence to prove what you have contributed. If you are unable to meet the payments, you should have urgent talks with your lender. They may be able to reduce your payments or provide a payment holiday for a couple of months to ease the transition. If arrears have built up but payments can be resumed, the lender may agree to spread the outstanding debt across the whole of your loan. Another alternative may be to alter your mortgage, changing the type of repayment option or extending the length of the term, although these options will depend on your age and financial circumstances.

If you are married and believe you are entitled to a share in the value of your home, consult a solicitor about registering a charge on the property with the local Land Registry office to ensure that your spouse cannot sell the home or re-mortgage without your consent.

Limit any damage

If you think you may be about to break up with your partner, there are steps you can take to limit any financial damage:

- Generally speaking, you're not liable for your partner's – or anyone else's debts – unless you signed an agreement or acted as guarantor.

- Make a list of any joint finances. If you've taken out a mortgage, credit agreement, a loan, or have a bank account in joint names, then you're both liable – jointly or individually – for the full amount of any debt. This is known as 'joint and several liability' and also applies to rent arrears on joint tenancies, arrears on joint mortgages, council tax payments and water charges on properties that have been jointly occupied.

- If you take out a joint mortgage then you'll be jointly and individually liable for the debt. Talk to your lender straightaway if you think there'll be a change in financial circumstances. It's crucial to keep in touch with your lender so that they'll view your circumstances sympathetically if you need their help.

Debt after death

When someone dies, debts are recoverable from any assets or money left behind – what is known as the 'estate'. No one else has to pay for the debts unless they are already liable under the terms of the original agreement and the debt is in joint names or someone has signed as a guarantor. Creditors have to wait until the estate is sorted out, then ask for payment. You may have to negotiate payments to avoid losing your home if the house forms part of the estate and could be sold to pay the debts. However, if it is clear that there is little or no money in the estate, write to the creditors and suggest they write off the debt.

13

Understand your
credit record

Companies that lend money through credit want to know whether you are a good risk – in other words, whether you are likely to pay the money back. Whenever you apply for any kind of credit, the paperwork you fill out will state that the credit card issuer or loan company will contact a credit reference agency to check your financial history and notify them that you have applied for new credit. By signing the form, you give your permission for the company to access your credit reference files, also known as 'credit rating file' or 'credit record'. In the UK, these files are held by three credit reference agencies: Equifax, Experian and Callcredit. They collect millions of pieces of information every month. This is sent to them by financial institutions such as banks and credit card issuers. They will also receive data from shops and commercial businesses that are licensed to offer consumer credit on anything from mobile phone deals and store cards to 'buy now, pay later' offers. The credit reference agencies do not make any judgements about whether or not you should have the credit; they help credit issuers and lenders to share information.

When you consider that there are currently more than 100 million credit, debit, charge and store cards in the UK, it makes sense to have some kind of central point of information so that lenders can make responsible judgements.

What is in your credit reference file?

Compiled from credit applications you have filled out, your credit reference file will typically contain your date of birth, current address, recent previous addresses and confirmation that your name and current address appears on the electoral roll, which allows you to vote.

There are details of credit accounts that were opened in your name or that list you as an authorized user (such as a spouse's credit card). Account details, which are supplied by creditors with which you have an account, include the date the account was opened, the credit limit or amount of the loan, the payment terms, the balance, and a history that shows whether or not you've paid the account on time. Closed or inactive accounts, depending on the manner in which they were paid, stay on your report for up to six years from the date of their last activity.

Credit reference agencies record an inquiry whenever your credit report is shown to another party, such as a lender, service provider, landlord or insurer. Inquiries – also known as 'footprints' – remain on your credit report for up to two years. There will be a note of your past and present applications for loans and credit (and whether or not they were successful) plus a record of any history of missed or late payments for loans and credit.

Additionally, the file contains information about arrears, defaults, county court judgements (CCJs) and bankruptcy. These are matters of public record obtained from government sources such as courts of law. Most public record information stays on your credit report for six years.

There are other problems that can haunt your credit rating file. Credit referencing will take note of anyone with whom you share joint credit – including mortgages. If your partner had, or still has, financial problems, the negative associations can affect your credit score, even if you have a perfect track record.

MYTH: Those shoes are in the sale so they are a bargain. I am actually saving £45.

FACT: No, you are spending £60 that you don't have.

Why you need to see your credit reference file

The information in your credit rating file is very personal and has an important impact on your financial life and on your ability to get credit. It is essential that you see a copy of each file to ensure that the information held about you is accurate. This can also help you to identify any issues that may prevent you from getting credit.

Some lenders only use one credit reference agency or supply varying levels of detail. Therefore, it is important to have access to your credit file from each of the three agencies to make sure that you are not being hampered by the black marks destined for someone else, possibly with a similar name, or penalized for applications or defaults that have never occurred.

To request copies of your credit files in the UK, you can log on to the credit reference agency websites for further information (**www.equifax. co.uk**; **www.experian.com**; **www.callcredit.co.uk**). You can use the computer in your local library if you don't have one at work or home. You can also send off for copies in the post (see Part 5 for details and addresses). The minimum fee is £2, but there are various online packages that allow you ongoing access to your file over longer periods and which will help you to keep a closer eye on your rating. If you do not have a credit card and are unable to pay for an online service, you can apply for your file by post.

Sort out errors

Check your files for errors and if you find any, follow them up. There are three steps you can take if you have incorrect information on your file:

1 Write to the credit reference agency asking them to either remove or change any entry that you think is wrong. Explain why you think the information is wrong and send any evidence you have that proves the information is incorrect. The agency has to tell you within 28 days of receiving your letter if the information has been corrected, removed or if they have done nothing. If the information has been corrected, you'll get a copy of the new entry.

2 If the agency doesn't reply, or tells you they've done nothing or makes a correction that you

don't think is satisfactory, you can, within 28 days, send them a 'notice of correction' to be added to your file. A notice of correction is a statement of up to 200 words written by you. It should explain clearly why you think the information is wrong or misleading.

3 If the agency doesn't reply to your letter enclosing your notice of correction within 28 days of receiving it, or the agency has refused to add it to your file, you can appeal to the Information Commissioner. The Commissioner works for the government and is responsible for enforcing the Data Protection Act. This protects people against abuse of any information that's held on computers.

You can find out more on the website:

www.informationcommissioner.gov.uk

Or contact via post:

The Information Commissioner
Wycliffe House
Water Lane
Wilmslow
Cheshire SK9 5AF

Keep your credit record healthy

We looked at cutting down on credit in Chapter 11, and ideally you should avoid having and using credit cards, loans and overdrafts. Yet there may be times when credit is useful or, in the case of getting a mortgage, it is essential. This section looks at how you can keep your credit healthy and gradually repair any damage done by your past debts.

MYTH: It's only one glass of wine, or maybe two, to be sociable at lunchtime.

FACT: Yes, but they are large glasses and at £4.90 each around four times a week, that adds up to nearly £40 a week (or more than £2,000 a year) not to mention a drink problem.

Credit checklist

Your credit chances are healthy if you can tick all the boxes below:

❏ I'm on the electoral roll.

❏ I've been registered on the electoral roll in every previous address.

❏ I pay my credit bills on time.

❏ I don't have any arrears.

❏ I'm in full-time employment.

❏ I've been with my employer for more than one year.

❏ I don't have any county court judgements.

Q. Why have I been refused credit?

A. There may be many reasons for this. If you are in debt or have missed payments on credit you already have then other lenders may not be keen to lend you more. It could be that your credit record does not have enough information. Get copies of your record from the main reference agencies to help you spot problems.

Why will one credit company refuse you and another accept you? The lenders are not keen to share their credit scoring criteria with the public, and rating systems can vary a great deal between lenders. Once they have your information from the credit reference agencies, some look for one or two pieces of basic information. For instance, if you are not on the electoral roll, the credit company will believe that there is a chance that your address is not permanent, or – worse still – fake. This means that the company has no way of finding you if you are late with payments or run up your credit limit and disappear. After all, who wants to lend money to someone they may not be able to find? Requesting copies of your files will enable you to spot crucial gaps like this and rectify them.

Too little or non-existent credit can be as much of a problem as no fixed address for lenders who are looking for customers who will run up large debts. Generally, unless you have any obvious financial horrors, such as bankruptcy, you should be halfway to receiving credit if you appear on the electoral roll.

If you find your applications are being turned down, avoid going from lender to lender hoping to be accepted. Every time a lender checks with a credit reference agency, it shows up on your file. To a lender, these 'footprints' can indicate that you are over-extending yourself financially, being refused by other lenders and forced to look elsewhere, or that a potential fraud could be involved.

There could be a good reason for your credit problems. If you have late or missed payments, loan defaults or CCJs, the details will be recorded on your credit file for six years (unless you pay off a CCJ within the first month). These may prompt a lender to turn down your application for credit. Nonetheless, if your debts are in the past but you still cannot get credit, there are ways to repair your dented record. Resist the urge to try to make everything better overnight and to throw good money after bad – credit repair companies can charge anything from £50 to £200 but there is nothing they do that you cannot do yourself for free.

The UK credit reference agency Equifax confirms that scores automatically improve as your overall credit picture becomes better. This means showing a pattern over time of paying your bills on time and using credit conservatively. In addition, you should focus on the red and amber warnings in your credit analysis provided with your file. These represent the main areas where you are not receiving maximum points. You can gradually make your credit rating healthier by:

- Paying your bills on time

- Getting up to date and staying up to date if you have missed payments

- Contacting your creditors or seeing a legitimate credit counsellor if you are having trouble making ends meet

- Paying off debt rather than moving it around

- Gradually opening new accounts when you need to and paying them off on time.

Understand 'bad' credit cards and loans

If you have had financial problems in the past, you may find it hard to get credit. Anything from late and overdue payments on previous credit deals through to bankruptcy can create black marks on your credit history. These are then taken into account by anyone you apply to for new credit.

The best way to rebuild a healthy credit record is to become debt-free and gradually take on small amounts of credit and manage them responsibly. There are no quick fixes.

What to avoid

Ideally, you should avoid credit, especially if this was your route into debt. If you are determined to get a new credit card, bear in mind that there may only be a few on offer until your credit record improves. The drawback is that these cards will come with a very high rate of interest – probably around 40 per cent. The rates are higher because the borrower represents a risk to the lender – if someone has poor credit because they have had problems in the past, the card issuer is taking a chance that the borrower may not pay off what they owe.

The other temptation that may come your way is from companies offering loans or goods – such as furniture or cars – to 'bad credit' customers. It may boost your confidence to know that someone is prepared to lend to you or give you credit on a desirable item. In reality, there is bound to be more in it for them than there is for you. The details could be hidden in the small print and may involve very high interest rates that will load you up with expensive debt. Another method is to get you to sign a secured loan so that your home is at risk if you do not keep up repayments. This is to be avoided at all costs. Imagine being forced to sell your home to pay off a loan for a car. Don't sign, however tempted you may be.

If you are tempted to borrow

Read the section in Part 2, Chapter 6 (page 73) about loans sharks and alternatives such as credit unions.

Alternatives to credit

A much more sensible alternative to expensive credit cards and loans are the pre-paid credit cards. These work very simply. You have a card account and pay cash into this before you are able to spend that available balance, using your card in the same way as an ordinary credit card at the same outlets. Most pre-paid MasterCard and Visa cards look the same as credit cards so you will be the only one who knows it is pre-paid. They are available from specialist online issuers and you can manage your account online or by post.

Nevertheless, you need to be aware of the downsides. In the UK, these include:

- A one-off set-up fee of around £10

- A monthly fee of around £5 or a fee each time you 'load' the card with cash; this could be a problem if cash is tight in the first place

- ATM (automatic teller machine) fees for withdrawing your cash

- Not being able to walk into a branch

- A time delay in making electronic payments to the card.

On the plus side, you pay no interest and do not accumulate any debt. Your credit limit is completely under your control and you can have as high a limit as you wish, as long as you deposit the cash to meet it. Plastic is a safer way to carry cash, particularly if travelling. It also gives the flexibility to pay for things online, over the phone and where cards are accepted. Best of all, it can help you to rebuild a better credit record.

> If you must have plastic but don't want the risks, pre-paid credit cards give you more financial options and help you to repair your credit history over time and with careful use.

> **MYTH:** *You can't expect me to cancel my gym membership. It's an investment in my health.*
>
> **FACT:** It would be an investment if you ever used it.

14

Help your children learn about debt and money management

Learning about debt and how to manage money is the best way to help your children to avoid borrowing and to start saving. Research shows that the current generation of teenagers is the richest there has ever been. British 16-year-olds earn more pocket money than ever, but they don't tend to keep track of what they are spending and they don't understand the difference between a debit and a credit card.

It is not just parents who are unhappy about this. Teachers are worried about the lack of knowledge of money management among teenagers. Financial capability is on the UK's national curriculum in schools but it is often mingled with subjects such as maths and social studies and may only be taught for 20 minutes a week.

A good start

Learning to save from as young an age as possible is important – children aged three or four can start with a piggy bank, and all the major banks and building societies offer special children's accounts. When birthdays and Christmas come around, encourage your childre to put money into their account and let them work out how much they have. Banks and building societies don't actually let children take money out until they are around 11 so there's plenty of time to learn good habits.

As well as savings accounts, there are friendly society tax-free bonds where you can invest up to £25 a month for children. They can watch the money grow and generally they cannot take it out until they are 18 or even 21. The UK government is helping children learn about saving. Those born after 1 September 2002 are entitled to a minimum £250 in the Child Trust Fund, which they can watch grow over the years as other money is paid in and they can collect when they are 18. Once children learn to save, they can build up a rainy day fund to tide them over and which will help to avoid the temptation of putting money on credit. Children can also learn from being given pocket money, which you might want them to work for. For instance, if they do certain jobs around the house, they get paid, so learn about the value of working for money.

Be a role model

You should be a role model to your child. If they see that you always use a credit card, they will think this is the way to pay for things. They need to learn that credit has to be repaid and that you will pay interest on any money you borrow. Children need to be taught to keep track of spending – to keep a note of everything they buy so that they have a running total in their head of the money they have left. As a result, they learn to manage their money and to see money as something they earn and manage themselves.

Teach your children to put money aside for short-term saving, long-term saving and spending. Give them an amount in coins easily divisible by three, and three containers in which they can divide the cash. From small beginnings, they can learn and avoid the worst excesses of the current debt generation.

I had no idea how much my bad money habits were affecting my family. My wife and children had all noticed that I was stressed and anxious. I would hate to think that my behaviour has been a role model for my children. Now I talk to them about saving more than spending.

George

15

Avoid debt in later life

It's important to avoid debt throughout your life, but it could become even more of a problem once you stop working and your income is reduced. Most financial companies will avoid offering large loans or lots of credit to people who are retired because their incomes are limited and they may not be able to repay what they owe. You should bear this in mind if you are approaching retirement and relying on, or planning to rely on, credit. The other way to avoid debt in later life is to ensure that you review your budget to take account of the changes in income and lifestyle. If you have not started saving into a pension or are not sure if you are saving enough, you should take steps to change this and invest as much as you can afford.

Why do I need a pension?

Put simply, a pension is a retirement plan designed to provide a secure income for life when you stop working. You may ask why you need to bother with a pension: the fact is that it would be a mistake to rely on the State to provide you with enough to live on – the tiny amount it currently pays to pensioners may not even exist by the time you retire.

We are living longer and healthier lives, so it is even more important to think about how and when to save for retirement. Retirement can last for 30 years or more. Depending on how luxurious you want your retirement to be, you will need to set aside cash now to fund everything from living costs to round-the-world adventures. To provide additional encouragement, the Government gives us a tax break on the money we save for retirement.

When should I start a pension?

It's a myth that you can be too young to start a pension. The sooner you start saving, the better off you will be because your pension savings need a chance to grow over time.

When working out how much you should save, think about the lifestyle you want when you retire and calculate how much you can afford to contribute towards your pension fund each month. You should also consider when you want to retire, and whether you have income from other sources. Typically none of us can afford to save as much as we ideally should, so just put away as much as you can as soon as you can. Regular reviews are important – keep an eye on how your investments are growing (or not) and how well they suit your circumstances and plans. You will probably need the help of an independent financial adviser at some stage. Talk to your employer about whether there is an occupational or stakeholder pension available and whether there is any help from them in joining or contributing to it. Occupational pensions are usually very good value, so find out if your employer runs a scheme before you look into any other options.

Part 4:
From the
Postbag

16

Your letters

Letters written to *This Morning* are completely confidential. These created letters are typical of the hundreds I receive each week.

Dear Denise

I have got myself into an extremely bad debt situation. I feel so ashamed and embarrassed about the problem. I even feel that I could end it all rather than own up to my own stupidity. My husband is very careful with money and he knows nothing about this. He is so kind and I don't want to hurt him. He has supported me through such difficult times before and he doesn't deserve this.

I have four credit cards and three loans. The interest alone is more than I can afford and each month it gets worse and worse. I can't see any way out of this and I am terrified that my husband will leave me if he finds out, but I am not sure I can keep this from him forever. I am so desperate. Please help.

Dear X,

I am so sorry to read about the problems you've been having. I can understand entirely that the debts you have accumulated are the source of a great deal of stress, and it's no wonder that you're feeling so desperate. And while I can appreciate why you might have wanted to try and keep this situation to yourself, I imagine that the burden must be almost overwhelming. Since the debt advice companies rightly point out that in order to continue managing your debts you will require an income, I think you are going to have to consider telling your husband. You say that you have a close and loving relationship, so would his initial shock not give way to understanding? If it were your husband who had incurred these debts, would you not prefer that he were honest with you, so you could both shoulder the responsibility? When you married you vowed to support each other for better and worse, for richer and poorer, and although neither of us can predict his reaction with any certainty, it seems more than likely from what you tell me that your husband will stand by you. Apart from anything, I would think that you can't hope to keep the real reason a secret indefinitely. Moreover, if you fail in your repayments, it's possible that you have far more to risk in the long term with regard to the assets you share. I know how difficult it will be to tell him what has happened, but at least then you can both begin to work towards a repayment scheme, and you can stop suffering alone from the acute anxiety and sense of dread you describe. However, it might help to talk to someone before you talk to your husband. If you have a clearer idea of how you're going to get out of debt, your husband will be less angered than if you are still uncertain of what to do next.

I would suggest that you contact the Consumer Credit Counselling Service (freephone 0800 138 1111) as soon as possible. You will be able to talk to a qualified debt counsellor who will review your circumstances free of charge and suggest courses of action that should help to make your financial situation a little more manageable. If creditors are aware that the counselling service has been involved, this can be enough to reassure them of their debtors' commitment to paying their bills, and they may be more understanding and patient in their handling of the situation.

I hope this helps a little. You can always write to me again if you like and let me know how you're getting on. In the meantime, you are in my thoughts, and I wish you all the very best.

Dear Denise

*I wanted to write to you and tell you how I pulled
through a terrible time in my life.*

*Two years ago I was made redundant and I
buried my head in the sand with regards to the huge
debts I had built up on credit cards. For months and
months I couldn't even pay the minimum repayments
and I would just try to swap the balances around to
keep the companies off my back. At this point, I owed
around £35,000. I was too scared to add the total up.
The day came when I completely ran out of credit and
couldn't swap the balances around. I was absolutely
petrified. I had no money coming in and I didn't
know what to do.*

*I ignored all the companies for a few months as I
just couldn't face what was happening. I barely went
out and used to physically shake all the time. Finally,
I plucked up the courage and wrote to all the
companies to whom I owed money to explain my
situation. Mostly, they didn't care – all they wanted
was their money back. I felt so alone and I seriously
considered suicide. Then someone put me in touch
with National Debtline, and when I spoke to them it
felt like a huge relief. They drew up a re-payment
plan and slowly, slowly I began to take control of the
situation. I still owe a lot of money but I can now*

*manage the payments and know that it will be okay.
My attitude to money has changed completely – I am
no longer scared of it, nor does it control me. I feel on
top of the world now. I feel free and alive again.*

*It is important to know that there IS light at the
end of the tunnel. However bad things look there can
be a way out. Please tell people to talk to one of the
free debt helplines. Sharing was the most important
thing I ever did.*

Dear X,

The last few years must have been horrendous,
and reading your story I could conjure up what
it must have been like waking up each morning
and having to face the nightmare of your ever
increasing debts. No wonder you became so
desperate. The decision to seek help was a brave
and sensible one, and now you're reaping the
benefits. Well done. You can see the way
forward and are happy once again. When your
life is back on track you'll look back on the
moment when you asked for help as a real
turning point.

17

Your stories

I felt very low when my husband left me and guilty about what it was doing to the kids. I realize now it was stupid but at the time I just kept buying things for myself and them, to make up for being miserable. Now I'm in so much debt with catalogues I don't know where to turn. There's no way I can pay it back and I'm frightened for my kids if I go to prison. Sometimes I feel like ending it all and taking the kids with me.

Angela

Angela was advised to contact the Consumer Credit Counselling Service. She followed their advice and now, although she still struggles to make ends meet, she no longer feels hopeless.

I got in with a crowd who had more money and better jobs than me. I suppose I was flattered that they let me. Anyway, I couldn't keep up but I went on spending, taking loans out and buying everything on tick. Now I owe £25,000 and the worst thing is that my job depends on me looking like a sensible person, which I now know I'm not. The only way out I can see is another loan to pay everything off but I've tried two places and the rates are sky high. I also owe my mother money she can't afford to lose and that makes me feel ashamed because she trusted me. I don't know what to do.

Matt

Matt was advised not to take out a consolidation loan. Instead his adviser helped him to make an arrangement with his creditors, whereby he paid off his debts at a rate he could afford.

We sank my partner's redundancy pay into a business and mortgaged our house, which we had owned outright, to make up the difference. It was madness because neither of us really knew enough about running a business. We tried to hold on but now everything is gone, including the house which we both worked years to pay for. My sister has let us move in with her but I know she won't put up with us forever and she's fed up of people knocking on the door demanding money we haven't got. I sit and think about how it could all go so wrong in four years. How can we start again at our age and anyway, who is going to trust failures like us?

Jean

Jean was advised to contact Shelterline (see page 243) about her housing needs, and both she and her husband now have a rented home and jobs. Although it will take time to restore their fortunes, they can see the way ahead.

I used to pride myself on being good with money but since my divorce I can't seem to manage to cover everything out of my salary. I've got a lot of debt, most of it on credit cards and some with a loan. I also have a mortgage on the flat I bought, which I now know was too expensive and it has swallowed up the settlement I got from my marriage. At the moment I'm just keeping on top of it, but I know that sooner or later it's going to get out of hand. I've cut back until I'm practically living on cornflakes and tea. Life is total misery and I only have myself to blame.

Pat

The answer for Pat was to sell her flat and buy a smaller one in a less expensive neighbourhood. She is now steadily paying back the money she owes and her outlook is much brighter. She hopes to take a short holiday soon, her first for four years.

I got some things from a catalogue and they just kept on offering me things, things we really needed but couldn't afford. Now they're threatening to take me to court. My husband doesn't know and he'll go mad if we get bailiffs in. Am I responsible or will they take him to court too?

Lila

Lila has not yet told her husband about her debts but she is working with a counsellor to work out a plan for repayment. This means that when she tells him she can also show how the problem will be solved.

*I went into partnership with a friend
who had a taxi licence. He told me we
could make a lot of money so I gave up
a steady job and put up money for
vehicles and a Portakabin office. He was
leading me up the garden path; the
money wasn't there and somehow I
seem to be responsible for most of the
debt we're in. Now I'm driving for
another company but the money is
nothing and I am hounded day and
night for what I owe. I used to think
bankruptcy was a shameful thing but
now it seems like my only option.*

Tony

The answer for Tony was to seek legal advice
about his partner's responsibilities in the winding
up of the business. Although things are still
unsettled, he can see light at the end of the tunnel.

I was so deep in debt I could see no way out. And the shame I felt was worse than the debt. I once calculated it would take 20 years to get back to being solvent again. I rang the National Debtline in despair after I saw it mentioned in a newspaper. The minute I made the call I felt better, just to know I was doing something. Now, after four years of taking their advice and tackling things, I can begin to see my way clear. I even bought a book the other day, the first 'treat' I've had for ages. The real treat though is waking up in the morning and not feeling dread about the day ahead. That's as good as winning the lottery.

Bridget

Bridget worked through her problem and deserved her treat. There will be more to come as she leaves debt behind.

Part 5:
More Help
at Hand

18

Your debt-free progress

Parts 1–4 have provided a huge amount of information for you to take in. Try not to feel overwhelmed and don't expect to remember all of it. Use this book as a reference guide for specific areas – as your lifestyle changes, it will make sense to go back to certain parts of the book if you need a reminder of practical or emotional steps and options.

Your budget

One thing that will benefit from regular reviews is your budget. You don't have to wait for any major changes in your life. Now you have done your budget once, it should be easy to dust it off and check your progress as often as you like. Use it to keep a close eye on your money – you will feel so much more in control and the budget will help you to avoid slipping into debt again. To begin with, you may want to look at your budget once a month because there is so much going on. You don't need to become obsessive about it, but once you have control over your finances, it makes sense to keep hold of that control.

If you slip off course

Life has a funny way of distracting us from all sorts of things. You may take your eye off the ball and find that you have used your credit card or overspent. If you have, don't worry. It's not the end of the world. Don't use this as an excuse to say that you are giving up and that you may as well stay in debt. You deserve better, especially after all the hard work you have put in. If you have made progress at a slower rate or been better at some things than others, that's fine. It's not a race. Here are some ideas that may help when you feel you need to get back on track:

- Write a list of the things you have done to become debt-free. You may be surprised at how much you have actually achieved. This will also help you to identify any gaps.

- Now note the areas in this book that you think you have not covered properly, not understood or not followed through.

- Revisit the relevant sections in this book and work through them in your own time. You may need to leave a few days in between each one if you feel you are taking on too much.

- Make notes in the book to remind you that a section has been covered or write down anything that still has to be done.

Don't be upset if your financial picture is not changing as quickly as you hoped. So much of the way we manage and spend our money is down to our lifestyle. We may need to make important changes over some time to make a difference overall.

The top ten steps to get out of debt

Do you need a quick reminder of what to do?
Here are ten ways to make a difference.

1 If you have more than one debt, start by
   arranging debts in order of priority. If you are
   struggling to pay your mortgage or rent or
   other living necessities, such as utilities, these
   shortfalls should be given urgent attention. If
   your debts are from loans, credit or store
   cards, rank them in order of the highest
   interest rate first.

2 Draw up a budget that will allow you to see
   how much money you have left at the end of
   each month to spend on debt repayment.
   Writing down details of what you spend will
   also enable you to see where you could cut
   back or make sacrifices and help to control
   future spending.

3 Switch to a cheaper credit card and you could
   take advantage of one of the many 0 per cent
   interest balance transfer offers to give you a
   breathing space. You should aim to stop using
   your card altogether until the debt is cleared,
   but if you know this won't be possible, pick

plastic that also has a 0 per cent introductory rate for purchases so that you are not adding to the problem. Make sure you cut up your old card so that you are not tempted to use it now that it is balance-free.

4 Cut up any spare credit cards or store cards to avoid temptation and write or call the companies to cancel your account. If you don't do this, they will reissue the card when it expires and you will find it hard to resist.

5 Speed up your repayments if you can. The sooner you repay your debts, the less they will cost you. The minimum payment on your credit card may look like an easy way out but if interest is mounting up, getting your finances straight will take forever. If you are paying off a loan, watch out for penalties if you try to repay it early.

6 Make the most of your income by saving money on all your bills where possible. Move your mortgage if you are on your lender's standard variable rate. Instead of lining your lender's pockets, the money you save on your monthly payments could help reduce more immediate debts. Switching your phone, gas or

electricity providers could also deliver more cash. Websites such as www.uswitch.co.uk will tell you the cheapest providers in your area, based on current usage. Your mobile phone company can also advise on cheaper tariffs.

7 Increase your income by taking on overtime or an evening job if possible. Spring clean your home and sell unwanted clothes, CDs, books, electrical goods and pretty much anything you don't want at a car boot sale, garage sale or on a reputable auction website such as ebay (ebay.co.uk).

8 Avoid debt consolidation and debt management companies. There is nothing they can do for you that you cannot do for yourself for free.

9 Keep talking to your creditors. They will find it hard to be sympathetic if you ignore their letters and calls. Lenders are used to dealing with requests for payments to be reduced and interest to be frozen, so you may find they can help.

10 Seek advice from a free debt counselling service such as Britain's National Debtline or the Consumer Credit Counselling Service.

How far have you have come?

	strongly agree	agree	disagree
I am more confident with my money.	☐	☐	☐
I know there is no point hiding from my finances.	☐	☐	☐
I am more confident with money matters generally.	☐	☐	☐
I believe I can now keep my finances under control.	☐	☐	☐
I believe I can get myself out of debt.	☐	☐	☐
I believe I can avoid debt in the future.	☐	☐	☐
What I have read has explained many financial issues to me.	☐	☐	☐
I feel prepared for my financial future and ready to adapt my money to changes in circumstances.	☐	☐	☐

If you scored 'agree' or 'strongly agree' throughout, congratulate yourself on your excellent progress and success.

If you scored any 'disagrees', look back at the chapters of the book that will help you in the areas where you feel there may still be gaps in your knowledge.

Good luck

Good luck with your money. Be proud of yourself for taking the steps to become free of debt. We wish you a very happy and healthy financial future.

19

Helpful organizations

Advicenow

Advicenow is an independent, not-for-profit website providing accurate, up-to-date information on rights and legal issues. It has information on the Living Together Agreement.

www.advicenow.org.uk

British Bankers Association

The UK trade body for banks that has useful guides and information for bank customers.

www.bba.org.uk

Building Societies Association

The UK trade body for building societies, which provides useful information for customers.

www.bsa.org.uk

The Citizens Advice Bureaux (CAB)

CAB helps to resolve legal, money and other problems by providing free information and advice from over 3,200 locations in the UK. Consult your phone directory for your local office.

www.citizensadvice.org.uk

The Consumer Credit Counselling Service (CCCS)

A registered UK charity that assists people who are in financial difficulty by providing free, independent, impartial and realistic advice. The CCCS can assess your situation and ask creditors to freeze interest, stop penalties, accept a longer repayment period and sometimes a reduced sum.

Tel: 0800 138 1111

www.cccs.co.uk

The Council of Mortgage Lenders

The UK trade body for lenders. It has an excellent website full of useful information if you are buying a home or already own one.

Tel: 020 7438 8956

www.cml.org.uk

Credit reference agencies in the UK

Call Credit
Consumer Services Team
Callcredit plc
PO Box 491
Leeds LS3 1WZ
www.callcredit.co.uk

Equifax
Credit File Advice Centre
PO Box 1140
Bradford BD1 5US
www.equifax.co.uk

Experian
PO Box 9000
Nottingham NG80 7WP
www.experian.com

Energy Saving Trust
Information and advice on how to conserve
energy (and reduce bills).
Tel: 0800 512 012
www.energsaving.org.uk

Energywatch
Energywatch is an independent UK watchdog for
gas and electricity. The website contains useful
information to help save energy and money.
www.energywatch.org.uk

Financial Ombudsman Service
Consumer helpline: 0845 080 1800
www.financial-ombudsman.org.uk

Financial Services Authority (FSA)

This is the financial regulator in the UK. Its website has plenty of useful information for customers and a database to check whether a financial company or person you are dealing with has the necessary authorization. The Consumer Information section has guides and comparison tables.

FSA Consumer Helpline: 0845 606 1234

www.fsa.gov.uk

Independent Financial Advisers (IFA) Promotion

IFA Promotion has been running for over 17 years and promotes the benefits of independent financial advice to consumers and businesses in the UK. The website contains useful information for customers and will help you find IFAs in your area and/or who specialize in a particular type of advice.

Tel: 0800 085 3250

www.unbiased.co.uk

Money Saving Expert
Martin Lewis, the original money saving expert, will help you save a fortune on everything imaginable. Sign up for his regular emails.
www.moneysavingexpert.com

Moneyfacts
Independent best-buy tables for dozens of financial products.
www.moneyfacts.co.uk

National Debtline
A telephone helpline for people with debt problems in England, Wales and Scotland. The service is free, confidential and independent. Specialist advice given over the telephone is backed up with free self-help materials and guides. The organization may also be able to set up a free debt management plan for you.
Tel: 0808 808 4000
www.nationaldebtline.co.uk

Office of Fair Trading
The Office of Fair Trading is responsible for making markets work well for consumers by promoting and protecting consumer interests throughout the UK, while ensuring that

businesses are fair and competitive. The website contains useful information and can help you avoid the latest scams.

www.oft.gov.uk

Ofwat

The water services regulation authority seeks value for customers.

Tel: 0121 625 1300/1373

www.ofwat.gov.uk

Payplan

One of the UK's leading debt management companies, Payplan's services are free. The company can help you to set up and keep to a manageable repayment plan for your debts and it undertakes regular reviews of your circumstances to ensure that your Payplan arrangement is still working. The arrangement continues until all of your debts are cleared.

Tel: 0800 917 7823

www.payplan.com

Shelterline

24-hour housing help.

Freephone: 0808 800 4444

The Samaritans

The Samaritans provides confidential emotional support 24 hours a day for people experiencing feelings of distress or despair, including those that may lead to suicide. They are there for you if you're worried about something, feel upset or confused, or you just want to talk to someone.

Tel: 08457 90 90 90.

Trading Standards

A one-stop shop for consumer protection information in the UK. Find your nearest branch in the telephone directory or go online.

www.tradingstandards.gov.uk

Unclaimed Assets Register

A unique search service that helps you to find your lost assets and to re-establish contact with financial institutions.

Tel: 0870 241 1713

www.uar.co.uk

uSwitch
A free, impartial comparison service.
www.uswitch.com

Which?
Which? fights for consumers' rights in two ways. It campaigns to make sure consumers get treated fairly and it publishes magazines, books and websites to help people make the right choices.
www.which.co.uk
www.switchwithwhich.co.uk
These websites give useful comparison tables and guides.

GLOSSARY

It sometimes seems that money has a whole language of its own. Here is a list of commonly used words and phrases and what they mean. If you are ever in any doubt about the meaning of anything to do with your money or debt, ask your adviser.

Administration orders In the UK, an administration order may apply if you have at least one county court judgement against you and your total debts do not exceed £5,000. It allows a county court to administer payments to all your creditors. One payment is made to the court and the court splits this between all creditors according to how much you owe. As long as an order is in force, creditors cannot take further enforcement action and interest is stopped.

Annual Percentage Rate (APR) Annual Percentage Rate is the number that gives you an idea of how expensive your credit card or loan will be. The APR tells you the rate at which you will be charged interest and helps you to compare one loan or credit card with another before you sign up.

Arrears Arrears occur when you fail to meet the contractual payments for your household bills. Missing payments for your mortgage, rent or council tax and so on can lead to serious arrears, which must be paid immediately. Arrears will accumulate if you continue to miss payments and you will be required to pay an additional amount on top of the regular payments until the arrears are cleared.

Asset An asset is something that belongs to an individual such as property, a vehicle, cash or shares.

Bailiffs Bailiffs are employed mainly by the courts. They will enter your property and take goods to sell at auction in order to cover debt that you owe to a lender who has previously issued a county court judgement that you have failed to pay. Bailiffs work under strict rules so make sure you know your rights when you deal with them.

Bankruptcy Bankruptcy is a legal procedure where a person who cannot repay their debts is formally declared bankrupt by the courts. The debts and assets of a person should then transfer to an appointed trustee. You or one of your creditors can petition for bankruptcy.

Budget A list of all your income and expenditure is a budget.

County Court Judgement (CCJ) A county court judgement is issued by the court to oblige you to make payments on a debt you owe when you have failed to keep to an original agreement with the lender and not made any attempts to come to an agreement of repayment.

Credit file A credit file is held by authorized companies and contains the history of your credit applications and use.

Credit limit The maximum amount you may owe through spending on a credit card is the credit limit. If you go over this limit, your card may be refused and you may also have to pay extra charges.

Credit scoring The system your card issuer uses to decide whether to provide you with a card and at what amount to set your credit limit is called credit scoring. It works by awarding points to the information you provide on your application form and to the information recorded on your credit report (held by a credit reference agency).

Creditor A creditor is an individual or a company that is owed money by another person.

Debt Any money that is owed or due to someone else.

Debt consolidation Debt consolidation replaces several loans or debts with one loan, usually offering one lower monthly payment over a longer repayment period. This is also known as a consolidation loan.

Debtor A debtor is someone who is in debt and is required to repay their creditors.

Default notice A default notice is issued by a creditor when a financial agreement that was made between you and your creditor fails because the arrangement has not been kept to. In the notice, the lender informs you that they are intending to take steps to recover the money you owe them.

Direct debit This is an instruction you give to your bank or building society to make regular payments from your account to a specific company. Unlike a standing order you agree that the creditor can vary this amount each month.

Final discharge A final discharge will be posted to you to show the end of your bankruptcy. This document means you are free from debt and the bankruptcy is over.

Hire purchase (HP) Hire purchase is the pre-agreed purchase of an asset where the asset is in your possession as long as repayments are kept to. Once full payment is made, the asset becomes your property.

Insolvency Having insufficient funds to meet all debts, or being unable to pay debts as and when they fall due, is a state of insolvency.

Insolvency practitioner A person who specializes in and is qualified to deal with insolvency, insolvency practitioners are recognized by the appropriate board and are fully qualified to deal with your insolvency.

Interest Interest (and interest rate) is the fee charged by a lender to a borrower for the use of borrowed money, usually expressed as an Annual Percentage Rate.

Joint account A joint account is a current or savings account taken out in two names, usually by couples. Arrangements can be made so that either individual or both signatures are required when writing cheques or when making withdrawals above a certain amount.

Joint liability The legal liability of two or more people for claims against them or for debts incurred by them jointly.

Joint and several liability When you take out a joint credit agreement with another person, such as a loan or overdraft, you are both liable for the full amount of any debt. This means that if your partner fails to repay the debt, the creditor could still ask you for payment of the full amount, even if it is money you have not personally spent.

Late charge This is a charge imposed by a lender to a borrower when the borrower fails to make payment on the due date. Look for details of whether these charges apply to your loans and credit cards – details may be in small print.

Lender A lender is a person or company that lends you money (usually a bank, building society or credit card company).

Loan An advance of money from a lender to a borrower over a period of time is called a loan. The borrower is obliged to repay the loan either at intervals during or at the end of the loan period together with interest.

Loan shark This is an unlicensed moneylender, usually charging an astronomically high interest rate on a loan.

Minimum payment The amount you must pay each month to keep your account in order is the minimum payment. Missing the minimum payment will mean that your creditor requests immediate payment and you risk a late payment charge being added to your account.

Official receiver (or trustee in bankruptcy) The official receiver (or trustee in bankruptcy) deals with the administration for bankrupt people. They will normally interview the bankrupt, and it is ultimately their decision whether assets should be sold for the creditors' benefit.

Payment protection insurance (PPI) An insurance policy that can pay an agreed amount if you are unable to earn because of illness or redundancy is called payment protection insurance. These are often sold alongside credit cards and loans.

Redemption penalty Lenders sometimes impose charges known as redemption penalties if you pay off your loan or mortgage sooner than expected.

Salary Wages received on a regular basis, usually weekly or monthly, are called a salary.

Secured loan This is a loan that is backed up by assets belonging to the borrower (normally property) in order to decrease the risk taken on by the lender. If you don't maintain your repayments, your assets can be at risk of repossession.

Self-assessment Since April 1996, all taxpayers in the UK are obliged by law to maintain records of their income and all types of capital gains to enable annual tax returns to be completed. This is known as self-assessment. In April each year, HM Revenue & Customs sends out almost 9 million self-assessment forms to taxpayers.

Standing order This is an instruction you give to your bank or building society to make regular payments from your account to a specific company. This is a fixed amount, whereas a direct debit can vary.

Tax credits Tax credits are tax you receive back in certain circumstances. For example, pension credit, child tax credit or working tax credit.

Unsecured loan An unsecured loan is where the lender has no entitlement to any of the borrower's assets in the event of the borrower failing to make the loan repayments. Such a loan normally carries a higher interest rate than a secured loan.

Also available from *This Morning* and Hodder Education are:

- This Morning: Beat Your Depression

- This Morning: Escape Domestic Violence

- This Morning: Beat Your Addiction

- This Morning: Get Over Your Break-up

- This Morning: Cope With Bereavement

- This Morning: Overcome Your Postnatal Depression

- This Morning: Cope With Infertility